A story of triumph following the experiences of one woman through the challenges life has thrown her way and a determination to live beyond them.

The synchronicity of unexpected happenings takes her to pathways that miraculously are just there, finding hope in ways that once she would not have believed possible.

This is a true story taking the reader to unlimited possibilities.

The loss of a son at sea, never to be found . . . the folding of a marriage . . . the end of financial security . . . all happening at the same time was almost overwhelming.

This true story chronicles a journey one woman has taken on a very jagged road, finding determination to holding onto belief in herself.

This book brings you to the joy of celebration . . . . of a life well lived in circumstances all too often contriving to derail her.

A book holding close to the butter-fly wings of Love

ABOUT THE AUTHOR

The Author holds a degree in Creative Arts from the University of Wollongong in N.S.W. Australia.

She is a Poet, Sculptor, Teacher, Student, Gardener and Mother. She now lives with her partner in a house she built with her own hands, on the edge of a rain forest, not far from the ocean where she found ways of living with grief through the darkest days.

Happenings empowered her.

Working with underprivileged young people—attending and graduating University—Teaching Aboriginal women—working at *Quest for Life*—all helped mould her into a stronger and more intuitive person.

The unexpected gave her strength.

A newly found sense of peace began to sustain her in writing this Personal Meditation, creating a celebration of life in all it's difficulties, to honour her son in his short life.

Grief is a River

A personal Meditation on being

fay marie mcdonald

For book orders, email orders@traffordpublishing.com.sg

Most Trafford Singapore titles are also available at major online book retailers.

Printed in Singapore.

ISBN: 978-1-4907-0160-8 (sc)
ISBN: 978-1-4907-0161-5 (hc)
ISBN: 978-1-4907-0162-2 (e)

Trafford rev. 10/18/2013

 www.traffordpublishing.com.sg

Singapore
toll-free: 800 101 2656 (Singapore)
Fax: 800 101 2656 (Singapore)

I walk in the world
and during the night
I dive into it
down to the bottom
underneath the currents
and drop my anchor

This is where I'm staying
this is my home

Bjork Gudmindsdottir

The sky is as blue as blue. The air is hot.

I woke this morning with an unusual sense of freedom for today is to be, completely mine, having let go a sense of foreboding of not really belonging to where I now live.

Crazy after a year of living here, and with Christmas but a whisper away, carrying endless possibilities.

I look beyond our bedroom to layer upon layer of inner city roof-tops, remembering a time, not so long ago, of living beside the river, watching the tide go in, and the tide go out, the nights dark and rhythmic, the rivers moods changing, flowing, nudging 'Feel Free' my sailboat moored at the end of our jetty.

Today almost tasting what life once held, living beside a river.

Thoughts as bitter-sweet as the seeds of a pomegranate.

Our bedroom has become my protective arm of quiet, where geraniums in the window-boxes are bursting with radiance as I lean out to cut away the few dead leaves burnt by the hot weather of the last few weeks.

What do I still need to do?

Did I ask John to pick up the wine?

There is something else, I know there is. I'm sure to have forgotten something. I always do and it is twenty past four.

Time to go down to the kitchen. Friends will be here between seven and eight. And then the telephone. With a handful of papery brown geranium leaves I move to the bedside table to pick it up.

I place the telephone back on the bedside table.

It's almost five.

Sunlight filters through the open windows. It hasn't rained for weeks.

Sheer white curtains billow out as if they were sails.

Again, the telephone.

It's John.

"What do I need to pick up, I mean is there anything else?."

"I'll see you when I get home, you're not hanging on to the argument we had this morning are you?"

"No.".

Julie's father said not to say anything, not to Julie or to anyone until he rings me back.

I lay by the telephone, my head resting on the soft pillow, the bathroom door is closed, the wardrobe door is open, clothes hang neatly above a jumble of shoes. My feet are bare. I must clean myself up, friends are soon to arrive, but this room will protect me for beyond this room everything is foreign, dangerous even. I don't want to speak to anyone, not until Julie's father rings me back.

The silence slips between me and . . . I am not sure what.

I look at my watch in a room that now seems unfamiliar, yet my bedroom has always been my favourite room, wherever I've lived.

Sun streams through the open windows. Geraniums a kaleidoscope of colour are glistening after the sudden sun-shower. It hasn't rained for weeks.

Even geraniums need water.

Startled again by the telephone. It's John.

"Yes, pick up cheese on the way home," I say.

Why is he ringing about cheese?

I remember, friends will soon be here.

"I'll see you when I get home," says John.

"Mum, are you deaf?" Julie shouts up the stairs. "I've been calling and calling."

Yes. I did hear her and it must be late.

"Mum, don't you have friends coming tonight? This kitchen is a mess. I'm off and out. I'm taking Zoe for a run in the park."

The rain-shower has passed. Julie is taking Zoe, our gentle giant of a dog, for a run in the park while it's still light.

That's what she's doing.

"I'll catch you later, Mum."

Yes, Julie will catch me later. I'll think about it later.

Julie's voice. Zoe barking.

A sharp slamming door.

Sounds from every direction leap out at me.

Standing by the window I look at the reds and pinks and shades of mauve and white geraniums in the window box, a tapestry I carried as little chopped-off cuttings from my home by the river, to transplant outside our north-facing bedroom window on the day we moved in.

Entering the front door of this house, you find yourself in a tiny welcoming entrance. To the right of the small vestibule you look onto a minute abundantly green courtyard, then you step down into the living room, then further down to the kitchen-dining-room, from where you look back to a larger courtyard. A space central to our home, rampant with ferns of all shapes and sizes and a mass of green ficus plants cling to the brick wall of the house next door.

The first day John and I walked into this house it had looked almost incandescent, summer beaming through an avalanche of never-ending windows, and walking down into the kitchen that day I knew this was to be the *heart* of what was soon to be ours.

From the kitchen rooms fan out, down to the sunroom and up four flights of a winding staircase to the topmost bedroom.

A house without a river.

I have to go downstairs. How can I leave my bedroom?

I have no idea.

Julie and me, John and Peter.

John and I bought this house after looking at many dreary inner city houses. We'd walked through the front door and in unison said 'We have found it.'

'Yes,' we had.

In the inner city, John and I had found the kind of house we had hoped to find.

Was it only twelve months ago that we walked into this house opening directly onto the footpath?

A no-fuss inward looking house turning its back on the outside world where my previous home had been open, entered directly from the river if you were visiting by boat, as many of our friends had.

A home, still as close to me as my shoes.

John and I now live in a street where trees bow sedately to one another across a wide black-tarred road. Stepping into this house on that day, there was not even a whisper of what our future was to be.

I have to go downstairs.

I have no choice.

Not sure why or what it is I'm supposed to do.

As I walk downstairs Julie arrives back from the park. It's six already.

Yes, she's back.

She's back and Zoe's barking

Friends soon to arrive will find their way to the kitchen.

That's the way it happens. Not a single person will move down to the sunroom leading to the back courtyard, or into the rest of the house until everyone is standing shoulder to shoulder. Only then will they make a move.

The kitchen-dining room is where it always begins. Why should tonight be any different?

But? Julie's father and I know just how different it is.

With Zoe scrabbling at her heels Julie rushes in to say, "John's home, weird vibes in this place today."

She gathers food off a large platter on the bench in the kitchen, ready to bundle it up to her room, where most of her time is spent these days.

"See you in the morning Mum. Angie is here, she's with John."

Julie's back to me, her voice muffled, stuffing food into her mouth, saying, "Angie and John are having a deep and meaningful in the living room, I'm staying out of the way."

Telling me Peter has gone to a friend's house, before rushing up the stairs taking two steps at a time to stop in the living room, jumping up and down in a frantic kind of rhythm.

Have you heard a word I've said Mum? Says Julie.

"Tell John his beloved son has gone to study with a friend. You really are weird today. Having a midlife crisis?" Asking in the hope of getting an answer. Anything would be better than the response she isn't getting.

Putting her plate on the table in the living room she moves toward the front door and with a devilish chuckle saying 'I'm going next . . .' but in mid-sentence she changes her mind, picks up the plate she has only just put down and, with Zoe at her heels, Julie rushes up the winding staircase heading for her bedroom.

I want to be beside our river.

Julie and I now live with John and Peter. I can't do what Julie does. I can't stay in my bedroom, yet today my bedroom is the only room I feel is mine.

Julie and Peter have their differences yet they band together as if they are warriors fighting the cruelties of what has been thrust upon them.

To combine two families has at times been anything but easy.

I stand in the kitchen on a day that has taken me way beyond where I now am.

Friends arriving move towards me, voices closing in are about to swamp me.

I can't do this, I can't My agitation peaks.

My friend Angie wanders downstairs from the living room.

"I saw Julie walking in the park with Zoe, she's all legs and arms at the moment, isn't she an amazing cluster of energies that daughter of yours?"

All I can think of is Julie, flames torching out of her nostrils, not comfortable with anything, or anyone, believing her father has deserted her. And he has. And yet not really, but his way of leaving had reduced Julie to a buzzing hive of inescapable feelings, Glenn, her brother, the only one who had understood just how fragile Julie was. Sewing herself into a coat of darkness, hidden behind a false bravado I had found almost impossible to penetrate.

The life she had been so sure of had fractured when her father left. In the blink of an eye, Fiona, her sister, was married in a park, and Glenn soon to leave and travel overseas. I now working full-time, needing to keep a balance by putting the recent past into the nearest cupboard, before throwing away the key.

I needed to move on, make a life for Julie and myself.

Before meeting John I'd gone back to study, then to full-time work. Two years later, having met John I sold our family home to buy this house with him in the inner city where I was now working. At times I doubt my move away from the river, the only home Julie could remember.

Then her brother flew away.

"A drink?" I ask Angie, who is still talking.

"John's worried about you. I am too. Where are you? You are completely strung out."

I'm trapped.

Everyone is crowding me. John on the other side of the kitchen is watching me.

I'm losing it, and John has no idea.

Where can I go to remember what I need to remember?

I can't do this. *Hold tight* I think. Then as if sleepwalking, speaking to no one, I make my way back up the stairs, past the living room, to turn robot-like and walk up onto yet another landing to open my bedroom door. The photograph of Glenn, Fiona and Julie is on the white brick wall, taken on the day of Fiona's marriage in an insignificant park in the centre of the city.

A park, important to both Fiona and Berndt, her partner.

The last photograph taken of them together before Glenn left for overseas, my eyes slipping past it to the open windows.

There is so much space out there.

I'm a long tall glass of tears.

I feel them. But I can't cry them.

Sitting beside the telephone, my hand rests on the receiver.

And the tears, it's as if they've been there forever.

It's a balancing act. I can't do it anymore. I can't.

John has followed me upstairs.

"What the hell is going on?" he says. "You've been acting like a zombie. What is it? What's wrong?"

I want to stretch out, I want to push John away, scared of what I feel. I want to move away. He loosens his grip, still holding me, arms stiffening waiting for an answer.

"Glenn's father phoned this afternoon," I say.

"So? What about? Why?"

"He talked to the Australian Ambassador in Sri Lanka. The yacht Glenn joined on the spur of the moment, the yacht he sailed on, they haven't been able to contact them. Robert is sure it's a mistake. The yacht probably had trouble with the radio, or lost a mast. There are all kinds of simple things that could have gone wrong. Glenn is a good sailor. Robert taught him well. He is sure it's a false alarm. I'm sure it is too. But John, what if it isn't?"

"My pregnant daughter is on holiday down the coast in your shack by the lake."

Fiona? Julie? What to tell them? What to tell Fiona?

"Her father has asked me not to say anything until he rings me back. The skipper of the yacht didn't leave a crew list. They are supposed to. They don't know for sure who was on board the yacht."

"That's the reason you weren't notified," John says.

"Robert is going to ring me back when he has news. He's frantic."

"John, what can I do? Nothing I've felt or done makes sense. I hoped his father would ring me back and say it was a stupid cock-up."

"He hasn't rung back. It could be a cock-up. Couldn't it?"

The house is quiet.

Not silent but quiet. John is downstairs taking care of everything.

Friends leaving a gathering that wasn't to be.

This was never Glenn's home, nor Fiona's, or Julie's.

Glenn sailed away.

Fiona's on holiday down the coast.

Julie's in her bedroom.

Friends going home without being fed.

God! I needn't have bothered, but I did.

Glenn can't be lost.

Mothers don't lose their children.

The sky goes dark.

The telephone rings and I don't want to pick it up. But I do.

Glenn's father's voice swims around me.

"Thanks," I say.

Thanks? For what?

Our son is out there. They don't know where.

Five young people and the skipper of the yacht *Crusader* are missing in the Bay of Bengal.

I don't belong in this house.

I want to drift above the trees, rise over the rooftops, reach into the blackness of a night sky, a sky that only hours ago had been pale and cloudy.

The geraniums are in the window box.

But not for me. Nothing is there for me

We sailed together once.

And, once only.

Glenn shortening the mainsail, me holding it firmly in the heavy blow, hanging out rather than in the boat, watching the water churn.

"Get your bum over the side," he'd yelled. No time to be polite when you're sailing in a stiff breeze.

"Keep your feet in the stirrups or I'll lose you. Here comes a gust, he'd called. soften the jib. That's it. We're almost there."

"One more tack and we'll be over the line."

And we did win that race.

It only takes a second to receive a simple phone call to find yourself in a space you hadn't known could exist, as if the earth beneath your feet had turned to quicksand.

Words unspoken sit inside my head. They keep on coming.

Way back living beside the river I needed to cut the ties between myself and Glenn's father, not wait for him to make a decision.

No choice but to do what I had to do.

Robert had not wanted a divorce. Yet, he'd moved on from our home to live with Christine and her three little boys.

He had refused to get a solicitor, giving me no choice but to send the necessary divorce papers to him through a process server. Then I asked Glenn, who was working with his father at the time, if he would be the messenger. Legally I wasn't allowed to give his father the papers.

Some stupid technicality.

Glenn left home that day with the papers. I must have sensed his dread at what he was about to do. With the surfboard on the roof racks of his slack Holden, he would have preferred to head for his favourite beach, the beach with the best waves thinking,

This is too f . . . ing hard.

But he hadn't.

Later, when Glenn was in Sri Lanka, I wrote to him about the time I'd asked if he would be the bearer of the legal papers his father hadn't wanted to receive.

He said he would. And he had.

How could I have asked him to do that? What was I thinking?

More concerned about how Robert would feel to receive them from a stranger than how Glenn would feel handing the divorce papers to his own father.

In the last letter I ever received from Glenn he wrote . . .:

> *Stop worrying about things you don't need to worry about Mum. We'll always manage to glue things back together, the way we've done with our boats. Use the glue to mend the worry you don't need to have. I'm doing just fine. Don't you fall apart. There is no need. Forget it. Everything broken can be repaired, often ending up even stronger. See ya round like a Roti . . . Glenn*
>
> *P.S The cover for my surfboard is holding up. It's great and the leather corners you sewed on at strategic points has saved the board from the rough handling received on the flights.*

In 1997, twenty years after the disappearance of the yacht
Crusader, on a clear sheet of white paper, this story began to
surface in fragments of memory, wanting to throw it in the fire
and not write about the loss of my son

Placed in a drawer, yet continuing to find its way onto the
page, and into my dreams that were often just shadows on my
eyelids, leaving me wondering . . .

What could they be about?

Scattering, wrapping themselves up in my head at night,
only to flee before my eyes were open. One dream had simply
been erased from my thinking as if it were chalk on a slate.

Way back, long before Glenn boarded a plane to fly away, one morning I woke, sure Glenn and Fiona were about to spread their wings, move on into what their lives were meant to be, often laughing together about what their future would end up being.

Conversations, that had never caused a moments apprehension.

Glenn would travel as he already had. Fiona was at college with friends who were already sharing a flat together.

That morning I sensed loss, an illogical sadness, and it made no sense.

I held it loosely.

I bought a scarf for Glenn to keep him warm on his travels, for Fiona a set of beautiful blue bowls from a shop in China town, not telling them why I bought these unexpected presents, but for me they diffused those three miserable days that had symbolized what I knew to be inevitable.

I still have Glenn's scarf. No idea what happened to the blue bowls.

Before long, Glenn and Fiona did move into their adult lives.

Not Julie, not yet.

As the busiest of beavers Julie had once said, "I don't want to play with girls, they don't do anything. Boys make things, do things."

Secretly, Julie at that age would have rather been a boy, for when she was quite young her belief was that boys had all the fun.

She loved her brother. As had Fiona.

It took years for Julie to move beyond wearing jeans and a particular shirt she'd patched creatively with her quirky embroidery, patchwork to express her tomboyish character. A shirt that could only have belonged to a girl.

Our everyday lives were being rearranged, and the future for them did become a reality, not just an idea to be imagined and planned for.

For those three desolate days, I wanted to clip their wings.

I wanted to freeze time.

There are days when I feel I've suddenly fallen down a staircase, not knowing it was there, to see pictures and words in the sweep of the sea. Waiting, still waiting.

Every time the front door opens I expect Glenn to walk up the stairs and into my bedroom. Sure he is out there, somewhere.

Wearing a purple shirt.

At night, the moon shining through the window, I sometimes reach out for what I can't get a grip on, falling asleep with oceans, islands and waves surging, rising and falling. Flares like opening flowers bursting above a churning sea, waking to the sound of birdsongs, to see the colours of a new day, thoughts of children bounding through their days. Glenn catching his first fish from the about to tumble-down-jetty the day we moved into our falling-apart shack by the river.

Sailing on the river. There always was water.

The three of them once roamed the waterfront, their brown bodies squelching, soft and slippery after the playful mud fights when the tide was low

Screaming out their joyful pleasures as only children can.

Bitter-sweet musings.

Nothing but the phone beside my bed is real. John makes the meals, he does everything. In my time away from work, who is doing the washing, the shopping for the food we need to eat?

John has a new car, a red Audi he tells me. Can I be excited about that?

Nothing can touch me beyond this bedroom.

I am not the only one to experience grief.

Good friends who are still living beside our river call into our home in the city.

They tell me the story of Joanne's father who had been picked up by the Germans for providing Jewish people with false passports in the Second World War, taken into custody by the Germans, and executed.

Eddie, barely a man, had been an underground fighter.

They had both known loss.

Spending time with me in my bedroom, not once suggesting I come out for a coffee, or a walk in the park, as other friends had.

They knew my thinking was where it needed to be.

With babies swaddled, rugs folded around them as if they were the petals of a flower, layer upon layer to hold them safe.

I had arrived unheralded at our holiday shack down the coast to tell Fiona the *Crusader* was missing, not believing Glenn could be on the yacht, hovering above it all, flicking aside the possibility that Glenn could have been sailing in a cyclone in the Bay of Bengal.

Earlier Fiona had been holidaying down the coast, shocked to discover she was pregnant, not sure how she felt about an unplanned pregnancy. Showering that morning she'd had a shivering sense of Glenn in trouble. Water rained down around her, discovering later that a May Day signal had been picked up by a radio buff in Melbourne. On that day.

The *Crusader* was having difficulty with everything battened down. Doing everything they could to stay afloat.

The *Crusader* had been missing since November.

This we discovered when Robert rang the Australian Consulate in the middle of December.

It is now late December.

It is now January.

A miracle for Robert to be given permission to search the islands east of India.

I scanned the papers for anything to do with Morarji Desai, the Indian Prime Minister, who was in Australia. And who had spoken to the press after a bomb exploded outside his Hotel in the city. The journalist writing that he was unconcerned about threats by terrorists.

They don't bother him.

"In life," he said "one has to get used to them. I don't think anybody can kill me if I am not meant to die." Pressed to explain, he tells journalists he believes everything is fixed, the manner place and time of death already appointed. I gather the terrorists who placed the bomb at the Hilton Hotel are not likely to disturb him. The main thing, he explained to journalists, was "not to be afraid," in fact he was quoted as saying,

"I am not afraid of anything in the world. I live only for the day, not thinking about tomorrow."

"Was life meant to be that easy?" a journalist asked, evoking hilarity with the press.

"Life is meant to be a matter of truth, complete happiness, and complete peace," is the response.

Desai fielded questions, throwing them back time and time again, moving nothing but his eyes. The journalists find him remarkably calm.

And peaceful.

Robert had flown to India. I sit in my bedroom.

I wait.

Ringing, writing, doing everything I can to connect the threads from around the world, while Glenn's father is out there searching.

Robert rings as soon as he has news.

A good idea contacting the Australian Consul in India, he says. The Director of the Home Ministry Affairs met me. He has already issued papers. He is going to be met at Port Blair on the Andaman Islands, the most settled in the Nicabar group. Desai had arranged a suitable boat, accompanied by one or two police officers.

It's a long time before I receive a telegram from Robert in the Andaman Islands telling me of an air search revealing traces of a yacht. Sighted in early December 1977 the wreckage appears to have drifted and will be picked up for identification.

My only connection now is to Robert in India.

The press in India had reported his meeting Desai, in Australia, soon after the *Crusader* disappeared. The day the meeting was to have taken place, the bomb went off outside the Hilton Hotel.

Glenn's father had been turned away.

Told by one of the Indian delegation to return the next day.

Desai, himself in the midst of chaos after the bomb had exploded, had given us permission to search for the *Crusader*. Agreeing to this after Robert was given an audience the day after the bombing. All previous attempts through Foreign Affairs had stalled, however the Indian delegation in Sydney had taken swift action when the *Sydney Morning Herald* journalist Graham Williams published the story of the yacht's disappearance, writing:

> Glenn had such a love of the sea that he interrupted
> a world trip in Sri Lanka last October to sign on to a
> 51ft yacht bound for Thailand and Singapore. Glenn
> an experienced yachtsman paid $200 for the fateful

trip. The yacht *Crusader* left Galle Harbour on a calm morning on November the ninth with six people aboard. It has not been seen after being caught on the edge of a cyclone in the Bay of Bengal. Its colourful eccentric Canadian owner, Don Sortie had last radioed the Crusader's position in November, midway between Sri Lanka and the Andaman Islands.

I had hoped the article would help with information leading to the yacht, needing to leave no page unturned. Reading it in print was difficult, but necessary and it had been newsworthy.

The journalist had gone on to say:

> Since mid-January they have made urgent pleas to India to be allowed to visit the Andaman Islands to search for their son. India retains a tight security around these Islands but permission has been granted.

The yacht left Galle Harbour. On board were Don Sortie, Judy Vaughn, a British woman who had been travelling with him, Glenn, and two other Brits, Stephen Bower and Rosemary Collier. At the time the article was written an unknown Californian was thought to be on the boat. I contacted his father. He flew out to Australia. He believed his son had disappeared travelling from Germany to India.

This young man's name was Danny.

On the eighth day out of Galle, a cyclone had arrived in the Bay of Bengal. It was the cyclone season. The yacht radioed they were encountering 70 knot winds.

That was the last message received from the *Crusader* by the authorities in Galle Harbour.

My days are made up of calls and telegrams to places all over the world, reaching out for information that could give a clearer picture. Letters to me through Foreign Affairs from ordinary Indians Robert had contacted, some from strangers, even to him. They had read about it in the newspapers. Simple letters addressed to Fiona, Julie and myself sent on from the Department of Foreign Affairs, one from a priest, Father Peter Gomes, of the Catholic Church in Port Blair in the Andaman Islands:

> Dear Mother of Glenn, Miss Fiona and Miss Julie. You will get surprised to get this letter of mine. You see I am a Catholic Priest working in the Andaman Islands for ten years as a Parish Priest. I am a Parish Priest in the Catholic Church.
>
> I came to know you through your (dad) (husband) who has come to these Islands in search of his missing son. On Friday Feb 24th the Daily Telegram have given the news, a father's search for the missing son. You see I met Mr McDonald at Calcutta Airport then he showed me your photos and of your son/brother Glenn. He gave me the entire picture of the missing son. Mr McDonald is going to the Andaman Islands. Dear mother and sisters of Glenn I have promised my help to you. I mean Mr McDonald, but our Indian Government has given him all kind of facilities over here. Mr McDonald and myself came to the Andamans by the same flight. I am here for the last ten (10)years. We too pray for Mr Glenn. I have seen your beautiful photo with Glenn. Hope to hear from you.
>
> Yours sincerely
>
> Father Gomes.

There are others. One from a man called Shavan saying

> *The Stella position indicated that he, your son is alive*
> *on an Island* situated in the northern latitudes from
> the place that was reported by your son. He has been
> well looked after, he is on the move and I for see
> you may have communication from him during the
> period from April 4th to May 30th 1978.

May the Lord bless this prophecy. Letters came, some
touching, others strange. Not ignoring the most unlikely
possibility we discover kindness and concern, in India, is alive
and well.

I am still in the bedroom, watching ants scurry one behind the other in the window box, my thoughts a cloudy grey film in a sullen sky.

Walking back from the window to the centre of the room, my footsteps muffled, and I can't bear to be anywhere but beside the telephone.

I read. I can't believe I can. But I do.

John was given Ayn Rand's books for Xmas. I have no idea why, but I'd started reading the first book *We the Living*, now I'm halfway through *The Fountainhead.* continuing from one to the other as if they're a lifeline.

They have taken me into Ayn Rand's world, a world way beyond my world.

I have no idea how.

In this room, by the phone, and in touch with Glenn's father I can hold it together.

I will continue to hold it together.

His father's latest letter arrives

It has been hard to get in touch over the last few weeks. It's taken three days to recover from the bitter disappointment of the aerial search to search the Sandy Islands, the mystic's choice. Not the yacht I had been hoping for. No S.O.S. No help. No x marking the spot on the beach. Nothing. On Tillanchong There was a mixture of exactly the same description the Americans had seen months earlier to the day. This means the debris had drifted 300 miles in 90 days against a consistently strong N E breeze. Possible. Every Island could support a shipwreck survivor. The natives travel long distances in their canoes, and the Indian Air Force has a regular reconnaissance because of trouble with fishing poachers. There is the picture as I see it.

A vague possibility, that Glenn is being cared for by natives. The search now is for a dinghy or any sign of survivors. I am hoping to leave tomorrow. A notice warning intending visitors to the Islands. Not allowed to make contact with the Islands small Negrito communities for fear of endangering their health with infections for which they have not developed any natural immunities because of their isolation.

I've had advice from a palm reader in Delhi, and a native hut dweller in Port Blair who does astrology. I had a séance with an old Indian Man that turned into a major comedy when he finally couldn't get a message through. Ending with a telegram from the Australian High Commission in Delhi to relate the opinion of an Indian man who swings pendulums. He says Glenn is west of here. The navy on the Island has an appointment lined up tomorrow with an astrologer, and a guest at the hotel is reading my palm tonight. When in India do as the Indians do. They are steeped in the occult, and mysticism from the top government official down. Very serious about it, so don't laugh. To date by all account Glenn is fine and he will show on a particular day in March. or soon after.

Perhaps it will be over by Tuesday. Thereafter we wait. And old Indian man who had been kind to Robert said, "What you can't cure. my son, you must endure. God is good."

Glenn's father is soon to return.

Being here and not out there searching, I am lost, but I will not give in to fear

How can I be here in my bedroom, doing nothing? Fiona and Julie must feel this too, but how would I know? I only know what happens in this room.

My bedroom.

Glad Robert is where he is, doing everything he possibly can, and constantly in touch. How could we have done nothing?

But can we do more?

Four young people, the skipper and his girlfriend out there in a windswept ocean.

Missing without a trace.

Yet today the sea could be like limpid glass.

I look beyond the pattern of the roof tops to emptiness.

I have been empty before but never like this.

That Glenn's father had left his family is true.

Is anything ever as simple as that?

Appearing to be leaving for somewhere, for some time. Not knowing where he was headed until he met Christine.

After leaving, his children were upset, particularly Julie. Back then Glenn and Fiona were moving beyond the early closeness of a family.

Their father had left me. He hadn't left his children.

He loves and has always loved them.

Growing up, their needs were no longer just within the family, they too were changing. Robert finding Christine with three little boys may have been a part of him wanting more of what he'd believed he was losing.

Now we have to face the unthinkable.

And John?

Standing apart, accepting, but in this he will always be the outsider for he had barely known my son.

This I know, my body feels it. All that keeps me functioning knows what is happening. I hear the shushing sound of a running hose. A bird whistles, Julie's cat Nimbus is watching and she jumps off the windowsill to land on the bed, wet grotty paws on the pages of my journal. A soft, gentle licking on the back of my hand.

Again, John will arrive home late tonight. I want the sun to shine.

Glenn had never felt sorry for himself, not the Glenn I knew.

I must bridge this yawning gap.

I no longer am who I once was.

Good times by the river are squeezing their way between the now and the what might have been. Rearing children beside a river we too had grown. Life was comfortable, and all had seemed to be known, happy times folded into the ups and the downs of building a life together that hadn't always been a silent battleground.

In 1975, when Robert and I were still living together, I'd applied for a job at The Smith Family Welfare Agency, saying to him,

"You have to make a choice, Robert. I won't live like this."

We had been on a see-saw for months. I was about to remove myself.

Maureen, my close friend, had presented a job application to me, demanding I apply.

"Time you got on with your life," she said.

Maureen's life had become a procession of doctors and hospitals, she was not having an easy time. Maureen had an inoperable cancer. Her time with us was unknown, making her determined to set me on a path before she left us.

Maureen. A feisty friend with a wicked sense of humour. A real friend, harassing me until the application had been written, and posted. Late applying, I didn't expect to get an interview. But I did.

Interviewed by a woman called Evon who called me the next day.

I held the phone, sure, even hoping she was to tell me I had missed out on the job. But I hadn't. I was to start work on Monday, realising how anxious I'd been about being successful in my application.

Yet to her I did say,

"Not only have you made my day, you may have made my year," hearing her laugh as I placed the telephone back in its cradle.

Glenn's father arrived home from the office that day, surprised to find I was about to begin working.

Returning to study, then to full-time work was like the sun shining through the blackest cloud, or rain after the longest drought.

Soon after this his father made his decision.

He left.

No longer living beside the river, that beautiful river.

I am in my bedroom, by the telephone.

Still waiting.

John is living in a forest grown dark, an alien in his own home.

The last thing he would have expected was for Glenn's father, Robert, to be involved in our life.

I not asking about his feelings. And John isn't saying.

He cooks, looking after a multitude of everyday things we've built around the differences of actually living together as a family.

Adjustments had to be made after taking the plunge. Buying a house together, scratchy things surfacing with little time to sort them out.

How are Peter, Amanda and Melanie, John's children, handling this? I barely know how Fiona and Julie are handling it.

I think of little else other than Glenn sailing on the *Crusader*.

Thoughts taking flight, thinking of Glenn as he was, not this loss of everything he will always be to me.

Twenty-three. An adventurous young man, always out there.

He would not want me to fade away, but be a candle, flicker back into life. Glenn would want me to do more than just survive.

To light a candle is simple. To bring light to darkness is natural. I want to see the world the way Glenn had seen his.

Fiona and Julie need me.

The breeze brushes my face. I need rain. The garden needs rain. Rain to bring renewal, and the breeze picks up, skating across the room to ruffle the papers on my desk, the green of the carpet is the colour of nature, that clever colour coordinator.

Who says blue and green don't go together?

I have a memory of a photograph.

Me as a young child in purple-spotted pyjamas standing on a beach, pyjamas blowing, clinging to my legs, a cheeky smile on my face on the day I ran away. Walking out of the house, and down the side pathway to climb over the fence when I could have walked through the open gate. For some wacky reason, only known to me. I just had to climb that fence and head for the beach that rimmed the bay.

At four years of age I'd wanted my freedom.

It's time to return to work.

Today, I'm having lunch with Sue at Bill and Tony's restaurant. *The No Name Café*

This is the cafe the staff have made their own, having an everyday conversation with Sue who has only just started to work with us, and she asks me what has seemed to become the inevitable question.

"Do you have children?"

"I have three, a boy and two girls." I've done it again.

"Is your son the eldest?" Sue asks. "Yes," I say.

"What's he doing?"

"He's overseas". Sue wants to know more. I use every means possible to stop the conversation, but Sue is on a roll.

Unremitting questions about where, what and how?

"He is travelling with a friend to Bali and beyond."

"What does he plan from there?" Sue asks.

"He was heading for London via Katmandu. Young men change their minds all the time. I can't say where he will end up."

My mouth is dry, thinking, *please drop it Sue, let it go. No more.*

Sue continues. "How often do you hear from him?"

Not believing what I'm saying, lie follows lie in fast succession, like some giant slug concocting a story about my son rather than telling it as it is.

This is like a slow crawl through wet cement.

"I have to get back to work," I say, "I have a meeting with David, he wants me to take over the front reception when I'm in the office."

I'm up and out of Bill and Tony's Cafe leaving the money on the table to pay for my lunch. Previously, having been asked what had become a not surprising question I'd said "I have three children and my son is missing at sea."

Telling this person the bald facts about Glenn travelling in Bali, then on to Sri Lanka, planning to travel across India, then to London, as if that was what he was still doing.

The friends he was travelling with continued with the trip they had planned without him for Glenn had wanted to sail the oceans of the world, and the Crusader was his chance to do just that.

"He rang to tell us he was signing on to a yacht. The yacht is still missing, in the last contact we had, he said he could be sailing into Sydney Harbour before we knew it."

"His father has been searching the Andaman Islands for a month."

"Nothing to be found."

The expression on her face had me apologising. I didn't even know her name.

"Sorry" I said, wondering what it was I had to be sorry about.

Everyday conversations could take me to places I could never have believed, rarely talking of Glenn, never knowing what to expect.

Loss howling across the ocean I couldn't bear to be near.

I was as barren as the salt pans of Lake Eyre.

There was a time I will never forget.

I met a woman called Sophie at a neighbour's Sunday brunch, asked the same question.

"Two girls, Fiona and Julie," I answered, followed by, "Sorry, I try not to do this, but I have three children. One, my son, the eldest of the three, is missing on a yacht with five other people from different parts of the world."

"The skipper. And a little white poodle."

"Missing, after a cyclone in the Bay of Bengal."

Sophie's hand reached out.

I looked down at her hand touching my hand, long slender fingers, a simple silver ring on her little finger, an uncluttered hand, her hand holding my hand.

Side by side we stood together still and quiet. The bustling sounds of children and chatter swirling around us that day was like snow melting in summer heat.

Sophie then saying in the softest voice,

" I know. My son was killed in a car accident. I know."

"We were able to put his body to rest. We know where he is."

And that was it.

And it was enough.

In the midst of a noisy brunch the salt pans of Lake Eyre had felt a little less bare.

Colourful poppies, primula's and the grasses in our courtyard, a pattern, images blending one with the other.

How can I applaud the life ahead?

Is death just another uncharted journey?

Is *Love* like finding water in the most arid of deserts?

I hear that there are plants that remain fertile for decades in waiting for rain.

An adaptability I now need.

Early in1977 Glenn had set out with his friend Lindsay to spend twelve months travelling to London, realising in Sri Lanka that the more they talked of Katmandu and London the more Glenn knew what he wanted to do. He wanted to sail across the seas.

He had no need of big cities in Australia.

Why would he need them anywhere else?

Just by chance Glenn had found an advertisement in a Galle newspaper.

The *Crusader* needed a crew.

It's February.

It's March.

April is almost over in 1978. More than six months since the *Crusader* was lost to us and the phone rings.

Damn, I think. It's Sunday. John is out and I don't want to talk to anybody today, yet I pick up the phone curious to know who is calling, even though I don't want to talk to anyone.

I could have told the caller on the other end of the line that I was sorry but I wasn't here at the moment. They could have responded with,

"Well then, where are you?"

I'm reminded of a line in a poem by Mary Oliver:

"If I don't know where I am, I hope I find my way back soon."

I could be having that conversation. I am definitely not here today.

If you were me you wouldn't be yourself either.

The day I read that poem it was as if I recognised what I was feeling in the words of someone else.

Today I am the poem.

Turning the pages of the calendar I circle the last week of May.

Been circling this calendar for months. No idea why.

Circling March and then April, now May is almost over then the doorbell rings.

First the phone, and then the doorbell. And I don't want to answer that either.

But I do.

Berndt, my son-in-law, is standing on the pavement, tears in his eyes, his excitement palpable.

"Kristian has arrived," he says. "Not Kristina. We have a boy called Kristian. He arrived two hours ago. I couldn't get here any sooner to tell you."

He tells me Fiona is tired, but she is also elated.

My daughter.

Glenn's sister.

Has given birth to a beautiful baby boy to be called Kristian Lief.

The sun shines. Trees dance. Honeysuckle creeps across the cement squares in the courtyard, surrounded by clover and small daisies pushing their way up through cracks in the paving. The musty cover of falling leaves takes me back to camping holidays, putting up the tents, and pulling down the tents, camping by the lake in the bush.

A breeze, the first caress I've allowed myself to feel for a long time.

Fiona, Julie and I take turns carrying Kristian in a baby carrier, called a Snuggli.

A kind of pouch. Carried this way he sleeps, resting against the beating of our hearts, going wherever we go. Out to dinner, shopping.

One day we even take Kristian to a movie.

With this close contact in the Snuggli he can sleep through anything.

After Kristian was born my thoughts streamed out like the tentacles of an octopus, not only thinking of Glenn.

But of Fiona and Julie. And now Kristian.

I remember the day Fiona and Julie, pushed Glenn out in his boat to sail in a race, both tumbled off the rocks to fall face down in the water, their brother laughing at them, gurgling, surfacing like porpoises. Julie screaming, it's not funny Glenn." Fiona saying, "When you clamber over oyster-covered rocks you should be wearing sandshoes.

"So what?" had been Julie's retort.

Glenn out there, sails billowing, aiming for a good position on the starting line.

Fiona and Julie climbing onto the jetty, heading back to the house to fix Julie's bleeding toe.

The nights sending me into a bleak confining space. A tightness in my chest that takes my breath away.

No way forward and no way back.

Trapped in the darkest tunnel by a nightmare, arriving unannounced.

Waking with my heart thumping, gripped by fear, as if a bulky overcoat is dragging me down, down, down.

Since the *Crusader* disappeared, Glenn is with me wherever I go.

He is my kite.

If I'm at work, or gardening, or playing with Kristian I imagine tethering the kite around my waist.

At times the kite wants to go further than the string will allow.

It's then that I hold it even tighter and, how curious it can be the way I come to little blinks of understanding. They come and they go. Sometimes surrounded by a gloomy apprehension, other times caught up in moments of grace.

In spite of this, or because of this, I am lighter.

But the nights. The nights.

Holding Glenn as my kite, and Kristian in his Snuggli.

I hold them both tight.

Sailing on the *Crusader* was doing what he wanted to do, yet Glenn was more complex in his quiet way than I had realised. His observations were different for a young man, and I was aware of this after reading the poems he'd left with me.

A private language, a part of my son that had surprised me.

He didn't label things. Certainly not people. That I had known.

Glenn had held a kindness of the heart, in his particular way. This I came to realise more clearly after one of his earlier trips to Bali. Before returning he'd given all he owned away to his Balinese friends, everything other than his surfboard.

What a dreamer. Material things were not important to him.

Never wanting to contain him, or expect him to do other than what he chose to do. And be. He knew what was important. There was little I could have said that would have made a scrap of difference.

I not only loved him. I liked the young man he was becoming.

A flashing like a faulty neon sign.

On off . . . on off.

Glenn no longer with me, yet here am I, imagining him as my kite.

Today everything in me is saying *No!*

As if I'm swimming underwater, not wanting to surface, in a race against time, holding tight to what I do not want to relinquish.

I must release him, and I don't want to.

For days it rains a torrent.

Not wanting to be separate from, not wanting to have lost him. Wanting him to slip back into himself as if he had never left, when he may need to move on to who knows where.

While I hold him here.

Yes, Glenn. I hold you here while you always wanted to be out there.

I am icy cold.

Do it. Cut the string to the kite that isn't there.

Days later the same nightmare returns.

No longer is it bleak.

The same, yet not the same in what now seems to be more a dream than a nightmare, raising my hands above my head as if to touch the softness of snow, drifting up and out of what had once trapped me, into a shimmering landscape in a light I'd never seen before.

Or since.

The nightmare has changed into a dream.

A yacht, sits there on the ice, on a morning as clear as glass, icicles on the stays reflecting tiny points of light, yet not a soul is to be seen.

I do not understand, not at first, then I begin to believe what the repetitive nightmares could be trying to show me.

Taking note of this gut feeling, knowing I have to find a way to symbolise the freedom Glenn always had when he was here.

In cutting the string to my kite, my heart and my body ache, and this is as painful as the day I was told the *Crusader* was posted as missing in the Bay of Bengal for in freeing my imaginary kite, I'd flicked a switch and the nightmare turned into a dream.

From that day the nightmares ceased to be.

I am never to lose the memory of the yacht balanced on the ice in the snow.

A still life.

I sketch the dream and its symbolism spills out onto the page of my journal.

In the silence of the morning, it am nowhere, light as air, as if dropped into a silent world. Since Kristian was born, there is an oddness. And it is strange.

To feel sorrow and joy side by side.

Last night a small box floated in as things do in dreams.

The texture etched onto the lid, a circle of indecipherable words, the box held closed by a small tarnished brass hook.

I search for a box like the one in my dream, finding it in a junk yard, costing all of three dollars, the junk-yard man telling me it was made by a craftsman, and that it was initially used to contain precious, delicate instruments.

I line the box with felt the colour of the sea and white feathers.

The box I paint as the bluest sky, adding the softest white clouds.

Felt, feathers and space to hold Glenn's last letters, his poems, his boat plans and the quirky notes he'd often left me on scrappy pieces of paper.

A note written on a piece of cardboard was left on my bed the last time he'd returned from Bali, found by me in the early hours of New Year's Day:

> Hi Mum, I had this compulsive urge to go down the coast to Swan Lake today. I hope you don't mind driving my car. I don't think my car is fit for the journey (no service stations open to pump up the tyres) Hope you don't really need your car today. I will ring this arvo or tonight to see if you want it tonight or tomorrow.

And on the other side of the tiny piece of cardboard was:

> Have a Happy New Year. Sorry for the inconvenience that may occur, but I had to have at least one day down the coast. See if I can still surf.
>
> See you soon
>
> Glenn

He was one of the original nomads, choosing to live an uncluttered life.

That's who he was. Never wanting the usual.

There is an article written by Ranjan Gupta in a New Delhi newspaper about Glenn's disappearance, titled, 'Paradise and Peril for the modern Crusoe.' The possibility being that he could be on any of the Andaman Islands. Many of these islands, Rajan wrote, are so far away from the shipping routes that a recluse might never be found.

A group of native fishermen and their women who had been stranded on one of the islands were found years later living off the island resources.

Children had even been born.

Last night I went to bed with the word *faith* buzzing in my head after watching a documentary about the Wailing Wall in Jerusalem. A holy Site from where Mohammed made his flight to heaven. A Jewish sacred site. A site of the Holy of the Holies in the Solomonic Temple.

Sacred.

Yet Jerusalem is surrounded by the irrational.

Is the Wailing Wall symbolic of the world's discontent?

I don't want to think about religion, man-made, and acted upon by man.

I think of Glenn driving down the coast after borrowing my car, taking it without asking, so desperately needing the freedom the sea could give him.

Thinking of Glenn, long ago on a roller-coaster ride at Luna Park, eyes closed, whirling through space, his adrenalin rushing at eight years of age, screaming out his happiness, wanting to go back on the roller-coaster ride time and time again.

It's been five years since the *Crusader* disappeared.

There have been days when the ghost of loss is with me in everything I do, yet there are days when life is what a four-year-old brings by just being there.

Everything today is as normal as it can be.

I am more part of the everyday, beginning to see and to feel, and more aware of what is going on around me, too often feeling like a wild monkey swinging through the tree tops, not sure which way is up, and everything around me is in disarray.

I ask John what is happening, his silence tells me nothing.

I live with questions, trying to topple the thoughts in my head into mad skittering nothingness, curled up in bed as if I'm living on the knife edge of my future, needing my garden and John is asleep, unlike me he can sleep through anything.

I need Nimbus and Zoe.

Yes. I need.

I walk out into the courtyard, a blue bowl in my hand, calling Nimbus, she rubs against the back of my hand holding the bowl, I rub the fur behind her ear with my other hand, she makes the usual curvaceous response to my gesture, stretching as only a cat can, then she licks the bowl clean before leaping into the garden to sit under a splaying palm.

Zoe joins us, sniffing the empty bowl before flopping down on the warm tiles. Nimbus makes her way over and begins to lick Zoe's ears and face, lick, lick, lick. This takes place every day between this cat and this dog, Zoe may be the larger of the two, but she's not in charge, and when she raises her head the cat ever so gently pushes her back down with a front paw. And the ablutions continue.

When the wall of glass doors are fully open, the sun-room is almost a part of the courtyard bordered by yellow daisies, roses and primulas, all peeping through the tangle of different sizes and shapes of native grasses.

All growing within a pristine, white-walled garden.

I always prefer a garden to be untidily prolific, but this one is a little like me, to contained.

Fragile though I may be, I am about to discover just how resilient I can be.

Walking back into the house, up the steps to the kitchen-dining room, reaching to the top shelf in the pantry I grasp the spout of a teapot that has sat there for five years.

Bought in a junk shop in Paddington. A quirky teapot, now a dusty teapot, not needed, or used, but it made us both laugh. We had to have it. Buying it the week we moved into this house, a teapot in the shape of a house, a present for our new home.

Leaning against the kitchen bench, I dread what this day is to bring.

Picking up the teapot, I look at it, then I smash it onto the floor holding myself together with an off-centre kind of stoicism, part fury and part knowing this is not meant to happen to us. Not to John and me. Not like this.

As John walks downstairs, I see our reflection in the glass door leading to the middle courtyard. I want to smash that image too, for this is the realm of the unbelievable. Yet I'd sensed it beginning, of course I had. John looks at the broken teapot on the kitchen floor.

In becoming real, it feels unreal, and I could not resist the erosion. I haven't known how to. John is leaving. He has packed his bags. I doubt I can handle this.

His silence is crucifying. Our life, the shattered shards of a teapot.

When I met John, all barriers to love fell away. My defences were gone, then two years later Glenn and five other people were lost sailing on the *Crusader* in the Bay of Bengal.

Our lives muted by my silent grief, becoming all too confusing for John.

Everything today has been the opposite of what I want it to be.

Ticking off the days in my head. Not on a wall calendar, writing pages to myself then cutting up bits of colourful paper that look like tropical underwater fish flying through the air. I want to walk away when I see myself coming, but I can't escape. I don't want to talk to anyone, their obvious concern seems to cause me harm, the opposite to what they intended. I don't want them to feel sorry for me.

I need to be myself in a way I have never been before. When I talk to myself no one can disagree or hurt me.

And yet, here I was welcoming a woman into my life after I'd participated in a program about healing. She and her husband were both central to the program and I so willing to be taken over by her charismatic personality.

Anything to feel alive again.

Before I introduced her to John I had thought of her as a friend, but after she met him she soon became too much a part of our life. Her sound, and her presence, became strident, like a strong wind over a sludgy pond, rushing, rushing, erupting.

Creating chaos as if her energy had taken John as a willing hostage.

It was I who had let her loose on our crazy fractured life.

I can pinpoint the day and the moment I knew for sure what had happened I walked into the house, I put my keys on the table in the hallway, and, looking down towards the kitchen my eye was caught by the ferns in the courtyard, speckled with the late afternoon sun. As John walked up the stairs towards me, I knew.

This was wrong, so wrong, then I was overtaken by a calmness in a situation that was strange, as if a cloak had been placed around my shoulders, offering me shelter. I almost felt sorry for John as panic coursed through me like a bolt of electricity.

Too late.

It had happened

Our love was as flat as a piece of tin.

On the radio Roberta Flack was singing, 'Beware my Foolish Heart,' while my world was spinning on a rickety foundation as if one leg was missing. The heart I had just begun to uncover shrank to the size of a pea.

For days I practise a kind of mumbo-jumbo I'd used years ago when I was far younger than I now am.

I would say to myself, if I put odd socks on I will not have to go to school today.

Or, if I sleep upside down in my bed with my dog Tangles on the right side of me I won't have a scary nightmare. If I ignore the girl at school who I want to be my friend, then she will become my best friend.

This thinking is far too crazy for a grown woman, but my requests now are so outlandish that they give me a weird kind of relief, like saying to myself, if the world comes to an end they will be the first to go. And I will survive.

Erratically I become more and more creative with what I wish for.

I have to stay focused, let go and do what has to be done.

But what to do first?

My friend Beth suggests I move down to their farm permanently, not just for weekends. Each day Beth becomes even more determined that I give the city the flick, saying,

"I'm not going to hold my breath waiting for you to make a decision. But there is no reason, no point in moving somewhere you hadn't planned when you can be here with us on the farm."

Could this be the way I move on?

And Kristian, what about him?

He has brought a balance to me that no one else could, restored me to a world I need to embrace. How can I create distance from him by moving out of the city, though it is only two hours south, an easy drive down the coast to what is known. Not unknown.

I see myself walking through the rainforest on the edge of the escarpment, Kristian trailing behind in his parka and his brand new gumboots, me guiding him in discovering things unfamiliar to a city boy.

I slide into fantasy. Kristian would love it.

I need to get out of the city, then I think, *dare I?*

Is what has happened to John and me, or what is no longer happening to us such a surprise?

For too long I cut myself off from everything but Glenn and the search for the *Crusader,* cloistering myself not only in my bedroom, but in my thinking.

After Kristian was born I did find ways to be a part of the world, though my heart and my mind were all too often still somewhere else.

And John the only one to know.

His walking out the door has unhinged me.

Has fate, that entity beyond understanding, called me to account, for I had left John long before he left me, and once he had loved me.

Get a grip on yourself, focus on what you need to do.

Not on what you might have done.

The day John walked out the door I had wanted to wail like a banshee, climb into bed and pull the doona over my head, discovering a few months later that our home was no longer our home. My last possession was about to be repossessed.

John and I were finished in more ways than I can count.

I thought of many things to say to John. I didn't say any of them.

I was too chilled.

Not by the few things John did say, but by his implacability.

It is so f . . . king unfair.

After another sleepless night I count every step down to the centre of a cold and uninviting house to sit on the bench in Bleaks-ville, chin resting on my curled up knees, needing to dismantle everything, pack it all into boxes, then take it to somewhere or to the farm.

I need to make a decision and do it. Take Beth up on her offer.

What have I left to lose?

I keep saying to myself *tomorrow I will think about it.*

I will do it tomorrow.

Finally realising I have no choice but to move out and to move on.

I wake this morning fuzzy in the head still thinking of Kristians' four simple words.

Does the world fit together like pieces in a puzzle, is there a plan to it all?

What could a four-year-old know?

The stars are in the heavens. We mere mortals live on earth.

I still can't separate what Kristian said from my jumbled thinking. His words keep going around and around in my head.

I can't talk about it, but I think about it all the time.

Glenn would have been the one to teach Kristian to skid stones on the river, to swim and to sail, all the things he'd loved as a boy. Skidding stones across the water to create circles that connect and separate the way people often do.

A four-year-old too wary to walk on the beach from the day he'd taken his first steps, let alone swim in the sea, bouncing up and down on the lounge beside Fiona and me.

Suddenly to stop and say . . .

"I drowned once, Mummy . . ."

Then to scramble across the room, and rush outside as if that had been the most natural thing for him to say.

And do.

His new puppy, Hans, struggling to catch up, had wobbled out onto the patchy green lawn, where sparkling fingers of water sprayed over a harmless battleground of a little boy's toys.

Kristian could have said, "I swam once, Mummy."

But at four years of age Kristian hadn't.

Frightened of the beach. And the churning of the waves.

Kristian was wary of the sea.

The sea, the sea, the sea will always be, in all I do, and dream.

Fiona and I were speechless that day and have remained so, hearing Kristian say . . . "I drowned once, Mummy."

I make my decision.

I am driving south.

I stop at the top of the escarpment, to see the suburbs of Wollongong sprawling below and, beyond the cluster of houses, the sparkling ocean winks at me.

Driving on, I turn off the highway onto the road leading towards Beth's village in the valley.

In my faithful green Honda I'm surrounded by a long line of black-and-white cows with soulful brown eyes, one after the other walking by, sniffing at my car window as if to welcome me.

All I can think of is digging the dirt in Beth's untamed garden.

I wind out of the village and up to the farmhouse. I climb out of the car and stretch.

Looking around me, I think, *I had imagined John and myself, one day, living in this valley, but this is not the way I had thought it would be.*

I walk along the curved pathway, but before heading up the steps onto the veranda I bend down to pick a rose off the rambling vine. I lay it across the palm of my hand.

I hold a bud beginning to open out. I want to open out. I want to see the past as if it were just a tracery of branches standing out against the sky.

Reach beyond the past, and beyond the obvious.

"Let the past be the past." Beth to me said.

"Drive south and make a life with us."

Yet when you have been living as if you were in a desert, you go at the pace the terrain will allow.

Is this valley to become my bedrock?

Can it define who I could still become?

Beth and I sit up late talking.

"Go for it," she says. "Go for whatever it is you need to do. Try anything. Take a step in a direction. You can have no idea what might happen."

I wake at the first light, and as long as it's morning I don't care what time it is.

I draw the curtain aside, watching cows roam past on their way back to the fields. Milked dry, they barge into one another like boats floating down a river.

A day will fall from a year. And leaves will fall from the trees.

I watch a tiny spider weave its intricate web. I need to be involved the way this spider is. Do more than let my days just drift away.

I'll drive up into the mountains. I'll drive out of the valley and up into the hills.

I'll not even think about where I'm going.

I'll jump into the car and drive.

Not a soul stirs as I climb into my car to wind back down into the valley, before I drive up the other side, to bump my way up the rough road to the top. A sign jumps out. A long time since I've driven up this road. Skidding to a stop I read the sign with a red arrow pointing to what is described as *a therapeutic community*.

It sparks my interest.

Turning off the main drag onto an even rougher bush track, I stop at a battered wire gate, nothing but scrubby bush beyond. A truck pulls up beside me. Young people skylarking in the back, pushing and punching, making a hell of a racket. I wind down the car window, and I smell and see liquid sloshing over the edge of an open drum in the back of the truck.

The smell is foul.

Sun in my eyes, I squint up at a blurred vision of young people.

"It's only silage for the vegie patch." They laugh at my discomfort.

"Why are ya here?" one asks. "Are ya gunna come in?"

"We'll wash our hands. I'll make you a cuppa," another says less stridently.

A tall man unwinds himself from the far side of the truck.

"Are you lost?" he says.

"No, but what's beyond the gate?"

"A refuge for young people," he says.

He repeats the previous offer, saying, "Come in and see what we're about. We'll make you a cup of tea."

The young people bouncing around the back platform of the truck are like unruly puppets on a stage, and they are mostly boys. I stop. They open my car door, ready to herd me up onto the veranda of a large old farmhouse.

"I'm David," the truck driver says.

Reaching out to shake my hand, formally introducing himself, taking care to just as formally introduce each of the young people before sending them to do their chores. It's a communal farm. A working farm to teach them the basics and the rhythms of the natural world.

"They now know where food comes from," he says with a cryptic smile.

"They get to learn about plants and animals, and eggs being collected, and animals being killed. They get to know what keeps us all from starving. Some for the first time."

Papers in a whirl scurry across the veranda, trees bend as if they're about to break, bringing a sharp stab of remorse.

Glenn is never far from my thinking.

Greg, the shyest, has stayed behind to make me a cup of tea. He looks as if life's not been worth the price he has had to pay. His stillness grabs at me. At the wire gate he'd looked at me unflinchingly, his eyes then slipping shyly away.

I smile as I thank him.

He hands me the tea with a biscuit, a cheese biscuit, then turns to rush down the wooden steps as fast as he can, heading for the safety of his peers. He's tall and thin.

Reminding me of the scarecrow in *The Wizard of Oz,* frightened of everything even though he'd found what he needed.

Greg is a few years younger than Glenn would have been.

His life must have been very different.

Yet at the heart of it could he be all that different from the boy I watched grow to be a young man?

David is talking to me.

"You'd think they were vying for a medal when someone new appears. It happens every time. They want to take you over, then piss you off when they get bored."

David's face holds lines of laughter, a wide-brimmed hat shades the warmth he has for these young people. I notice his uneven teeth as he pulls at his droopy moustache.

His weathered tan has the look of well-oiled leather, a man of patience.

If honest toil is a believable term, then David bears its mark.

Over another cup of tea I suggest working in the community for one day a week, mentioning I'd worked in clay. They have all the equipment.

"Many come to work with them with good intentions," he says.

"They come and they go as fast as summer rain, as fast as I can shuffle cards.

These buggers don't make it easy."

"They can be unfair when they put their mind to it, believe me you are a novelty.

They'll test you. They'll see if you can go the distance. To give you a cup of tea is a breeze."

Is their behaviour preparation for rejection?

Thinking to myself, *come on, jump right in, what the heck, what is it to drop one day from an empty week?*

Probably a challenge.

My decision has been made.

I've moved out of the city permanently.

I'll take on what I offered David now that I am living with Beth and her family.

I'll see what happens.

The weeks pass.

I do make progress.

Slowly.

But nevertheless I do progress.

The day is burning hot. The kids are going ape-shit, using everything they can to bring me undone. Today is to be a challenge.

Tuesdays, rain or shine, I drive up the mountain to work with these young people, every time imagining I'm holding an umbrella over my head to deflect their behaviour. And it has worked. My not reacting no matter what they choose to do has been a success.

Of a kind.

But today my not reacting is bugging them.

What do they want?

It's important to find a way, just as these kids have found ways to create barriers, by stepping outside situations. And yet I'm barely aware of the traumas they've had to live through that drives their outrageous behaviour resulting in their living in this community.

And it is unique.

Run by a group of people of the Rudolph Steiner Philosophy.

Their belief in what they can do for these lost young people is central to everything they do on the farm.

With my symbolic umbrella held over my head, the obscenities like rain are being toned down, sometimes even washed away, giving me the chance to do what I too can do.

But today my umbrella idea is not working. It has fallen in a heap.

"What'll we do now, Miss?" the ringleader from hell, Les, screams.

"If all you want to do is scream, fight and throw clay around," I say. "I'll just sit here and watch. I'll make a coffee. I'll leave you to it."

Damn the little varmints to hell and back. You need a hundred percent faith with zero doubt to work with these kids.

Some days they do surprise. But not today.

I don't want to give up on them but . . .

"You're all bloody shit-stirrers," Greg yells, "that's what you are. You all piss me off."

He's angry. Greg has never done that before.

"Don't call her Miss," he screams." "She told you, she's got a name. Use it."

"She's a missus anyway. She's got kids."

Les shrugs, retorting loudly as he throws a lump of clay out of the window targeting a tree. "She's the cat's mother, Greg."

The shrilling of the kettle cuts the atmosphere.

I pour myself a coffee, then in silence I walk out of the room.

It's almost lunch time.

Black-and-white birds scratch around under the fig tree looking for anything, anything at all. With no rain the grass is barely there. What's left is dry and brown.

What do I do, what can I do?

Sun drills into my skull, encasing blankness.

Greg walks out of the room and heads towards me, his footsteps muffled on the soft dry earth. Then he turns abruptly to walk off in the opposite direction.

I walk towards my car, climb in and drive down the mountain back to the farm.

"I'm not getting anywhere with these kids, Beth."

"Keep at it," she says. "You'll break through."

"How can you be so sure? No matter what I do it all comes to the same sticky end."

"That's rubbish and you know it."

I've been away from the community for two weeks. They have been told I'm to come back today.

All of them are impatiently waiting at the gate.

They open it and I slowly drive through. Some hang off the car.

Greg runs beside it. I find this confusing.

"We didn't think you were comin," shouts Les. "And yer late."

Today is different.

And that's not all. Greg is laughing, actually laughing. Not that I expect them to be well behaved but something has changed in the way they are this morning, as if they're saying, *Wait, please wait, we want another chance.*

Don't go. Not yet.

And I stay.

I need to succeed with them as much as they need me to not give up.

In my hand a lump of clay can become something else.

I've changed, working with these hedonistic young people.

I had no idea where I was going the day I jumped into my car trying to run away from myself, only to find I couldn't. Turning up at their gate and then being invited into the community.

And look at them now.

I needed all the strength I could gather to deal with these loquacious young hounds, chucking clay around to graffiti the walls when they were bored, then producing clay tits and bums and the odd penis. And little else.

"Look what I made Miss," Les says on the day I now call Deliverance Day.

"Another penis," is my response. "Aren't you clever, Les, why don't you make a whole row of them, keep on making them? Perfect your technique."

For just a second Les is stumped.

"Design them as a sculpture," I say. "Be inventive. You, Les, could be producing a work of art."

Fit to burst, his eyes popped.

"Yer up yourself Miss. Yer sick," he says.

That I enjoyed.

Greg has grown taller and stronger.

But is still melancholic at times. Where once I'd seen him as a scarecrow walking across the fields, now he is a robust young man, discovering his quick and quirky mind in a way I would not have thought possible.

I haven't given up on them. And they have changed around me.

Passing their test, Tuesdays has improved beyond belief.

They hang on to their clay monstrosities, though often tempted to throw them into the slurry bin. They begin to make choices by tossing what they aren't pleased with away, and trying again. Not always making tits and bums.

Together we make progress.

Eventually we go our separate ways.

To leave them and go to university is not an easy decision.

But it is right.

I need to do more than work one day a week.

I need to be taken over unreservedly.

I need to leave no space for anything else.

I had been talked into applying to the university by a young friend called Mandy who had short red hair with one long skinny plait down her back, swaying from side to side across her beige op-shop trench coat. Doc Martins keeping her feet firmly planted on the earth.

"I'm going to university," Mandy said. "I want to become a painter. I want to act and I want to sing. Why don't you come too?" she had asked with a glint in her eye.

And a smile on her lips.

"You'd have to be joking," is my reply.

Soon to find out just how determined Mandy can be, for only a year later my ending up at uni is totally unexpected. Not what I would ever have imagined myself doing.

So, I became a full-time student. Nothing to lose, and possibly much to gain. Having not the slightest clue what that could be. And I didn't care.

Beth asking, "What are you going to do with it?"

"No idea," is my reply.

"I am going to do it I'll spread myself around, on the edge of sadness, but I will be moving into a new and different landscape."

My second year at university is almost over.

Seeing John occasionally, thinking, *no I don't think so.*

Though my retreat from the world as I knew it is becoming less of an option.

So much now to take in. And do.

At university the young people had picked me up and carried me forward.

Being a full-time student as well as building my barn in the rainforest up behind Beth and Floyd's farmhouse has ended up being nowhere near as overwhelming as I thought it could have been.

My new barn-like home is almost complete. The interior almost habitable, but surrounded by rampant lantana, offering me little hope of creating a garden.

With the money left from the sale of the home John and I had bought in the inner city, I was able to buy this package barn. With my trusty pouch buckled around my waist I have nailed the last piece of rough-sawn-timber cladding into place.

In my bedroom at the top of the steep staircase are two doors that I myself had hung to lead out onto the deck.

Yet to be built.

French doors hand-crafted by Gino, my friend in the sculpture department at uni, and they were undeniably beautiful.

The building of the barn, along with university, has created a rhythm for me, spending weeks carrying the rough-sawn cladding up to the edge of the rainforest in light, but lengthy bundles.

A rhythmic walking meditation, a continuum, walking up and down, day after day.

Months ago this packaged barn had been unloaded beside the farmhouse. A conglomeration of different shapes and sizes. When it was delivered I'd asked Floyd, Is that all there is? Is there enough? Are you sure it's all there?

Bowie, the family dog, had not been happy that day, he didn't like change.

Where I had begun to welcome it.

Floyd carried this barn in pieces on a trailer at the back of his tractor, then he'd helped me bring it all together like a huge jigsaw puzzle.

Kristian, staying with me in the farmhouse the week the barn was delivered, had played around the edges of what was going on, following Farmer Floyd, as he had called him, wherever he went.

Floyd never quite sure what to do with the adoration Kristian so readily offered.

Having moved into my home, I want to let everything else go.

I live on the edge of the rainforest, and Beth and her family are but a breath away.

I do belong, I am meant to be here.

And I'm asleep before my head hits the pillow.

Waking early. I make myself a coffee, adding a spoonful of sugar, the spoon clinks against the cup as I place it back on the saucer.

I love the smell of coffee being brewed, but not so much the taste.

I make coffee for the aroma.

Finishing the last dregs, I place the cup back on the saucer and lean against the doorway, breathing in the sounds and the damp pungency of the rainforest.

Running my hand down the smooth timber framework I think . . .

I built this.

A currawong executes a mid-air swoop to land in a tree nearby. Perched on a slender branch, it fluffs its feathers, bouncing precariously.

Oh, to feel so light—yet be as solid as a rock.

This is the first week of living in the home I built.

So different from living in the city. And I laugh. It is just another year, another place, another time.

I had spoken to John before moving out of the farmhouse and into the barn.

He had offered to help and I had declined.

It was all too complex.

Not sure where I want to be with John.

He is so far outside of what my life is now.

We had once belonged to a world that had come tumbling down like a pack of dominos. One disaster on top of the other.

Doubting we could ever be as we once were. We'd zigzagged away and then back into contact, converging, but not connecting, my priorities were taking a different direction.

I had to remember all that had gone before, learn from it then let it go, for in the shadows of the now distant past so much had had to change.

In my third year of Sculpture and Textiles at university I'm working harder than I ever have, my concentration at times quite surreal.

I'm not always in control, yet I am giving full rein to my imagination, finding ways to express myself in clay, fabric, metal, in all kinds of materials.

And in my writing.

At university I've discovered there are no limitations.

The only limitations are mine.

My final year at university is almost over.

Against expectations, John and I have decided to live together.

But can I do this? Will we need a time of heavy sandpapering to reclaim what is still possible?

Even then we may need even finer sandpapering?

John has arrived with everything he owns.

His embrace is a light kiss on the cheek.

We have been living very different lives.

Now he is here.

John looks around at the space I've made mine, I turn to what I'm cooking for lunch. A piece of salmon skin side down with butter and a little of my favourite olive oil sprinkling a handful of dill into the pan with a squeeze of lemon juice.

The butter and the oil crackles as I throw a salad together.

Can we get it right this time? I think, *and can I handle this?*

John opens a bottle of wine, and pours me a glass, I look up and smile. Lifting my glass as he lift his. He reaches out, tentatively touching my shoulder.

Has there has been a price to pay for the happiness we had from the day we met?

I'm doubting my decision, for when John left I was like a sparrow without a garden, and I need a garden to grow things, create things.

I remember meeting John for lunch weeks ago.

"You look awful John," I said. "Good," he said. "I want it to show."

Thinking I'm far from perfect, and as charismatic as John can be he too is imperfect, even love is imperfect, yet we still feel it, in spite of everything. Together we have caste the rolling dice. We together have made a choice.

I'm taking a break today, surrounded by the sounds and smells of spring, its colour and its lightness. After weeks of rain, and now sunshine, the seeds I planted are beginning to sprout, the way Glenn sprouted, as he grew to be a young man living by the river.

Beside a river there are things to do.

We first explored that river in an old wooden boat belonging to an elderly couple,

Joe and Mary Hickman, who lived next door to us.

Soon after we arrived to live by the river, we rigged up a raggedy old tablecloth as a sail to float off down the river with the wind behind us All five of us on board.

Robert, myself, Glenn, Fiona and two-year-old Julie, then we took up the oars to row the boat home against the wind.

A steady row-boat, but not a proper sailing boat as it hadn't a rudder or a keel.

I now live on the edge of the rainforest.

No longer by the river.

To say that when one door closes another opens is a cliché, but for me, that is how it has been. I built myself a home that is just personal to me.

Maybe soon to become almost as personal to John.

We now live on this land in a house sculpted out of the earth and rocks and dark, rough, sawn cladding, nestling as comfortably as a cat into the shadows of the rainforest, looking to the mountains on the far side of the valley where a clear definition can be traced between the earth and the sky.

Layers and layers of green on green, a mantle of grace, a backdrop to the colours of the lichen on the limbs of the large stinging tree that rises from the deck.

No longer do I sit on the last train to nowhere, or drive as far as I can to escape myself. I stay awake. And I pay attention.

I've run out of endings.

His presence appearing in waves of memory.

Is this the beginning Glenn would have wanted for me.

Day touches night and warm touches cold.

And here I am. The four years at university have changed my life, this final year the most exhausting. I am a mature-aged university student, desperate to bring the installation I've been working on to completion.

There have been days and weeks filled with the joy of spending time creating, and not always successfully. The final installation is not coming together, and the essence beyond the facts seems to be eluding me.

I'm stressed. I'm running out of time. The closer the deadline, the more ballistic I become, and the more pervasive the chaos. *Trust the process. It will come together, it has to, this installation needs you.*

Focus on that.

As a last resort I look to my journal. Why not? No point avoiding it.

Time to pay a visit.

My final project is to be a celebration beside the creek running through the back of the university. There has to be water. There always has been.

A *Celebration* of who Glenn was, and still is, to me.

As a very small boy, my son was always himself. How did a small child have such a solemn dignity? Wild though he may have been at times in his teen years, Glenn had no trouble being who he was meant to be.

Glenn I now realise, was the balance in our family.

I miss his simple, uncomplicated way of handling so many things after Robert left, particularly with Julie. But that was a long time ago.

Focus on what I need now, find my journal that is kept in a box once belonging to my grandmother, filled with other musty memorabilia. Glenn's box is inside the larger box. I loved that box long before my grandmother died and left it to me. She had lived with us from when I was very young, and for me her box was magic. It held special things. And my wishes. Such as, if I was mad at my father, as I sometimes was, I would go into my grandmother's room, open the box and pour my anger into it, then close it and walk away, able to love my father until the next time I needed the box.

I haven't written in my journal for four years. Essay writing had taken over. Lifting the lid, I take out the journal and turn one page after another, thinking, *this is going to take forever.*

A date. January 7 1985. The dream I'd written in my journal:

> Glenn was there looking very light in colour, relaxed and happy. I was not surprised but I was excited. I had a new red car, and the car began to drive away. Glenn ran after it. The car was gone. I didn't see Glenn again, but he was there. We were on our way to a funeral. Fiona and Julie saying, You can come with us don't worry about not having a car. My shoes were not right. I was trying to find a suitable pair. They looked wrong. I went to get other shoes. When I came back Fiona and Julie had left. Trying to get a lift I jumped into a car with people I didn't know. I wanted to find Glenn. I phoned the people I'd bought the car from to ask if they would give me another. I didn't think it was normal for a car to run away, not a car on its own.

Glenn hadn't spoken but he was happy. Dressed in Indian-like colourful clothes. He hugged me and I wanted more.

With the journal on my knee I turn another page, almost the last, and I haven't found a thing that'll help with my installation.

Where can I go from here?

I need a coffee. I need a walk to the creek. I need, I need, I need.

Turning the page I find yet another dream. It looks as if a spider has crawled across the page. At the time I wrote this in my journal I was being creative as a mature-aged uni student, finding a more organic way of living. A new routine for me.

Yesterday I bought a small potted purple geranium.

The house is beginning to accept John, even better than I am.

I turn back to my journal, and there on the page is the word CELEBRATION?

CELEBRATION of what?

At the top of the page in strong letters dated January 10 1985.

Another dream but it is legible.

I have no memory of having written it down. Had it been too final.

How could it have been erased from my thinking, when before I'd had nothing?

I read it again:

> I say fare-thee-well Glenn. This I celebrate. It begins as a sad event. I am in India. There are many people and, I am dressed as a young bride. I sit at a table with two women in saris drinking champagne out of delicate glasses. Flowers floating in the champagne. One woman is saying we are to have wonderful food. We are to have a feast fit for a king. I'm back to the event still dressed as a young bride with bare feet. Fiona and Julie are with two other women. One a priestess of some kind is raving. We say that's not what Glenn would want. We want this to be the way Glenn would want. It's about who he was, we want this to be real. Flowers were floating in the

creek, and in glasses filled with champagne. Earlier I was sitting beside a coffin. Feeling sad. Not wanting to communicate with anyone. Foges, a close friend, sat down beside me saying, come on stop mooning around, this is a celebration. I was angry. Don't tell me what to feel or what to think. Sure he said that's fine. Then the coffin was gone. In its place, a blazing, warm fire. I, the barefoot bride wearing a coronet of flowers. I have been with Glenn. He walked away, leaving me, a young bride with bare feet.

Glenn will always be . . . twenty three.

The Celebration is to be beside the creek running through the back of the university.

There had to be water

There always had been.

This installation is the *Celebration* of Glenn's life.

Celebration Day. It has arrived.

An artist from the Netherlands, Jose, has been my supervisor for the project. She stands at the top of the steps leading down to the rainforest at the back of the university.

"Do I talk about what it represents?" I ask.

"No," Jose says, "you don't have to do anything. You have done what you had to do. Now take a deep breath, let go, just let it go, the installation has come together. I have travelled through your youth, your hopes and your loves. I have met them on every page, seeing them through your eyes. How can I mark you for this?"

"In the silence and between the words you have gained an inner strength."

"I celebrate you."

If I hadn't put pen to paper and written the dream down it would have been lost.

And here it is beside the creek. I don't want the space to be assessed.

I don't care what anyone else thinks. *Not today.*

Breathe deeply. Let your heart sing. Walk down the steps and into the rainforest.

Walk through it one more time before you share it with anyone.

I light the candles leading to the installation.

Twenty-three candles on twenty-three steps.

The box holding Glenn's letters is lined with blue felt and soft white feathers, and suspended from a tree. Floating free, standing out against the sky.

My clay footprints lead to flowers floating in the creek.

The essence of the installation is in my journal, placed on a rock, open at the pages on which the dream was written down.

In the creek, stepping stones lead to a table covered with a white, embroidered cloth, glasses filled with flowers, and champagne. The symbol of the barefoot bride is a simple white dress drifting out through the trees, a coronet of flowers holding a long floating veil.

Beyond the table.

Beyond the barefoot bride.

Beyond the champagne glasses filled with flowers is the funeral pyre.

Surrounded by twenty-three candles.

Beyond the bride drifting in the ether.

The Celebration begins.

At the top of the twenty three steps I open my car door. I turn on the music hearing it drift out through the rainforest. In my flying blind, the installation has come into being, often believing I had no hope of bringing it to completion, and the more exhausted I became, the more dismal the results.

I'd resorted to god knows what, and I'd pleaded to god knows who.

In turning the page, I discovered the dream.

For weeks I'd been filled with doubts of returning to the past.

Thinking, *Will I or wont I?* Becoming desperate in looking for anything.

In the journal I found what I needed most, unaware of it until the day I discovered the dream, held in a moon-glazed light, reflecting back to me what I had least expected, and giving me what I need to express the Celebration of Glenn's life.

It will always matter that my son is no longer here.

But there are nights when I'm able to tuck these thoughts under my pillow.

And sleep on them.

Abandonment, loneliness, we've all experienced one or the other.

I've come to accept that we are all alone. And will always be. To see this as clearly as I do now means my perspective can begin to change. Aware of the many small kindnesses, for there is nothing to fear, and much to be grateful for.

But this realisation has taken me a lifetime.

My days as a university student are over.

I talked to a student in the Sculpture department, who said, "You've finished your assignments and I'm way behind, can you take over my group of Aboriginal women and children working in Screen Printing at the Aboriginal Medical Centre for a few weeks till I finish what I still have to complete?"

I jump at this, saying, "I will."

I begin working with them in a garage and a tin shed at the rear of the Centre.

A time for me that is beyond description.

The women and the children have a wicked sense of the ridiculous. With their outrageous black, black humour they show me over the next seven years what real courage is, in spite of what has happened to so many of the first caretakers of this land. The land we the fair-skinned interlopers have so readily claimed as ours.

The first weeks it was difficult to find a way past the indefinable colour block.

Working with them, the line was crossed. I gain their confidence.

I trust them to make mistakes, and then to try again.

One day I place a long piece of material on the table, then I give each of them a square of screen printing paper. I ask them to draw. "Anything" I say.

"No way," they say. "We can't draw."

"We all doodle," I remember saying. "Like you talk on the telephone with a pen in your hand, you doodle don't you?"

"That's not drawing" they say. "Just make marks that's all you have to do. We'll play with colour. You'll understand. Trust me." I say. And they did.

They make their marks. Then I ask, "Who wants to start?"

Ruby of the loudest voice and the softest heart was up for it.

"Choose your colour, Ruby," I said.

"Design over design. You'll see. And you will be surprised."

She chooses red, laying the screen onto the fabric, pulling the paint across it with the squeegee. Proud of being the first.

"Repeat it," I say. Completely cover the fabric.

"What about the others?" Ruby says.

"That'll be fine. This is about colour over colour, Ruby."

One by one they choose their colour. Each layering the fabric with their design, one design over another. They learn more about colour, and design, and shapes than they believe is possible.

It becomes their prized signature piece.

Their entry into creativity. It wasn't complicated.

Having fun with colour over colour, creating a diversity of shapes, and shades.

Working together as a team, they are prepared to try anything.

These women and children sit on edge of my thinking in a way that is . . . unexplainable.

All I know is, that our time together is important to me.

And they know this.

There are things I want to do today.

Friends to catch up with in the city. My mother's birthday tomorrow.

I drive to the city to sit in a handkerchief-sized restaurant by Balmoral beach with a friend. I look beyond the heads to the ocean, then choosing what to have for lunch.

The sun makes patterns on the crisp white tablecloth. Children dig in the sand.

The water of the harbour leaks into the bluest of skies.

Sitting beside the sea I'm happy.

I lift a glass of wine to my lips, not even a sip and I collapse, slumped in a bustling restaurant, held in silence as my friend rushes away.

A tall man stands in front of me. Not hearing him, but by the look on his face he's telling me not to worry.

I'm cut off as if behind a sheet of glass, seeing everything but hearing nothing.

A young woman sitting at the next table looks at me then quickly turns away. Her romantic lunch is ruined.

Sorry, I think.

She watches as I'm carried out of the restaurant, placed in an ambulance and rushed to North Shore Hospital.

An artery had opened up, leaking into the right side of my brain.

A cerebral haemorrhage . . .

Arriving at the hospital I lose consciousness, later, waking to find John, Fiona and Julie beside the bed, and a smiling Irish doctor asking me a question. The answer, clear in my thinking, comes out as garbled rubbish.

She asks again, my response no different.

Silently I move my head from side to side. Not about to try that again.

Yet I feel not a scrap of fear to find myself so incapacitated.

But this thinking didn't surface until much later.

Here I am, totally wiped out, yet being in a state of peace that is unbelievable considering the circumstances.

I have no explanation for how clear and uncomplicated I feel.

Crazy!

John, Fiona and Julie, standing by the bed, and hearing my garbled response, must be appalled.

About to have lunch, and here I was being rushed to North Shore Hospital and wondering why my friend following in her car looks so stressed.

My body ceases to function, my speech becomes crazy and jumbled, my eyes unfocused, the right side of my body out of my control, yet I was in a state of absolute peace that is still impossible to describe.

I have every reason to feel fear. Yet I don't.

Later, I realised I'd been totally unaware that the odds were not in my favour.

My blood had flowed into all the wrong places before it stopped. A fraction of a second later and my body would have been beyond repair.

I'm placed in a darkened room, pushed and pulled, torches shone in my eyes, my toes tugged. The pain is excruciating.

But the pain does come to an end.

Next morning I am wheeled into a ward, happily disconnected from everyone and everything, held in a sensation, a feeling of pleasantly being outside time.

Concern for the shock others might be feeling hadn't even touched my thinking.

I have never experienced anything like it.

I am outside time.

I am where I am.

Nothing can touch me.

I just am.

Days later I remember my visit, only weeks before, to the Sunnarartum Buddhist Forest Monastery at Bundanoon to experience the putting together of a set of monk's clothing. A ritual that takes place every year, dating back to the time of Buddha, to provide a new robe for the monk most in need.

Sewing machines appeared, white cotton was cut and sewn. Everyone helping.

The completed white robe was to be saffron coloured using a special plant dye sent from Thailand.

In a large copper bowl the dying process was to be completed before the sun appeared.

The fire was stoked. Everyone had taken turns through the night to swirl the robe around the bowl with a wooden pole.

The simple joy of stirring a robe in a bowl had brought out the natural joy, and laughter the monks so easily expressed.

Part of a simple act.

A ritual from way back in time.

After my time in hospital I know the Monastery is where I will go, to heal.

I have no idea how, or when, this might happen.

But I know it will.

Before returning home, I am transferred to a rehab unit.

There I teach myself to walk, and then, and only then, do I agree to go home. Home at last, soaking up *The Miracle of Mindfulness,* a book I'd read in the rehab written by the Buddhist Monk Thich Nhat Hanh. Attempting the simple task of washing plates in the kitchen sink, mindfully squeezing the life out of my quiet, but indiscriminate thoughts, thinking only of what I am doing.

Washing the dishes.

John is in bed.

Wondering if I can return to work with my aboriginal students, hope fluttering like a caged bird, but John has agreed to take me to the Buddhist Forest Monastery for the meditation on New Year's Eve.

The end of the old and the beginning of the new.

Driving home with John, I have no doubt I am to spend time at the Monastery, saying to John, "What has happened has given me something I can't explain. I have to honour it, John, not sure how, but if I don't, I will lose what I've gained.

John is reluctant.

I'm not yet able to drive. To leave me sleeping in a Kuti in the forest, in a space only big enough to hold a mattress on the floor, a low table with a candle my only light, John thinks this is a little extreme.

But he has agreed to take me to the Monastery, then return three days later to collect me. For months this is to becomes our ritual.

A year later I return to the hospital to be assessed by yet another Neurologist.

The doctor is surprised.

Looking at what is written on the paper in front of him, saying, "What have you been doing?"

"I have spent time over the last twelve months at a Buddhist Monastery. I learnt to meditate."

"Looking at what is written on the paper in front of me" he says, "and I look at you sitting there. I can't believe what I'm seeing. All I can say is: whatever you have been doing, keep on doing it."

I am fascinated by ants, busy little creatures, I always have been.

I watch them trail along, one behind the other in a regulated line. Not put off by the unevenness of the peeling paint on the windowsill they climb methodically over the chipped curling edges, one behind the other. With no deviation.

As there is to be no deviation from me healing my body.

I hear a cracking sound in the rainforest. After the heavy rain a tree has come tumbling down, so loud it startles me, and probably bringing vines and whatever else with it.

Bush creatures will burrow into the fallen debris.

They will know what to do. They have their sense of order.

As my body once had.

A bird calls across the valley. Another in one of the trees. The bird in the tree rising from the deck seems to reply. The sound so clear in the silence.

This year the coming spring is different to any other.

The day I drove down the coast from the city to live at the farm, it was, as if I'd been walking on jagged rocks for months.

Chunks of my life, just slipping away.

To lose a child is like losing your life—yet you are still here.

The haze of loss permeates you. It takes a long time to find a safe space.

I had to do whatever I could do with my less than perfect life, reach deeper into it, leave the fake surfaces, and repetitive talk, and the weary roles we can all take on.

I want to slide into myself, find a way to just be.

In 1983 this wasn't a walk in the park. This was more like I was the head of a battering ram being hurled against a concrete wall.

I have been given the all clear from the neurologist. Now John and I are making plans to travel to London, then on to Ireland for six weeks.

Ireland was like going back in time.

So surprisingly modern in unexpected ways. I'm drawn to the gentle quirky ways of many of the people we meet on our drive west from Dublin, through the Burren. An amazing area made up of rocks, rocks and more rocks on the west coast of Ireland, to arrive at Spanish Point in County Clare.

There I find an other worldly simplicity.

Soothing to my spirit and my body.

This part of Ireland is bleak. And barren.

Its beauty is its starkness.

This isolation touches me with a language I need to hear.

Arriving home from Ireland.

I fall into a pit.

Having to accept that working with the Aboriginal women and children is no longer possible. I don't know what to do.

I need to be passionate about whatever I do.

Then I meet Linda at the South Coast Writer's Centre. I have never been a part of the centre in any way, but I have been receiving their newsletter since starting university.

Reading and writing has always been my tranquiliser.

My state of self-possession.

Linda greets me with, "Are you here for the workshop?"

"No," I say. "I'm not a writer."

"If you write, you're a writer," she says. "And if you are not a writer," she continues, "what are you doing at a writer's centre?"

Then she laughs as I say, "I've always written, but I'm not a writer. I called in today to check the centre out."

Linda talks me into staying to sip at what she is offering.

Later, I leave to call into the newly completed Aboriginal Centre.

Surprised to find it is their Opening Day and all of my former students are there.

Here I am, happy to be spending my days writing.

Something in me is changing, murmurings within me are finding a place to rest in the words, and the sound on the page, in the joy of being taken over. Being so passionate about what I am now doing day after day.

Yet this week I'm losing touch. The unexpected is all around me. I seem to be moving beyond what my writing life had begun to be.

My options had become unlimited after meeting Linda, and working with Sam, an effervescent young woman, the Director of the South Coast Writer's Centre.

Amanda John's daughter has returned from a year in Seattle. Rod her partner had taken up a residency at a well regarded Canadian Hospital, where Alexandra their daughter, their second child was born.

With what has been happening around John's family since her return, all I seem able to do is watch everything fall apart. Real communication no longer seems possible, so much has changed around his daughter Amanda since her return from America. Interaction within John's family is falling apart.

John wants to be clearer with his son Peter, Melanie and their mother.

Needing to share with them what Amanda is going through.

Is it impossible, to hope his family could pull together, not move further apart?

It's as if I blinked and threw myself off my shaky perch.

With all that has been happening I landed myself in hospital. Once again.

Later transferred from hospital to rehab, I seem to have moved beyond myself, the woman I really am, but at the same time I am more than a patient in a hospital needing to regain her strength, and once again insisting I go to the rehab unit before I return home.

The first night is like finding a brightly burning lamp when you have lost your way by casting yourself adrift.

What to call the night nurse other than surreal? She floated around me. Tea arrived without my being asked if I wanted tea. Milk, sugar, and even hot toast and strawberry jam in the middle of the night. You get used to cold toast when you've spent any length of time in hospital. The nurse left, returning armed with heated blankets, carefully wrapping and folding me into a warm cocoon of comfort.

In silence.

Tears close. *Rivers run clear, rivers run slow, rivers run deep.*

This nurse knows as if by osmosis the kind of silence I need.

She smiles, she smoothes my hair, gently tucking it behind my ear, then she turns off the light, kisses me lightly on the forehead, and closes the door.

Never to be seen again.

Words can so often be forked with meaning. Surprising and unexpected.

Yet it was the silence of an ethereal being, a night nurse, who had left me to weep with a relief I still feel.

After being in hospital and two weeks in rehabilitation, John is driving me home.

I am light hearted.

Not sure why, but a line in a T.S. Eliot poem that I have never forgotten comes to me.

"My life is like a feather on the back of my hand."

Gentle, delicate, words soft enough to feel the joy of my return.

The headlights of the car pierce the emptiness of the countryside. John is beside me, but my thoughts are of sailing on a river, slicing through the water, the pattern of slap-slap, slap-slap slipping past a smooth green fibreglass hull.

Feel Free painted neatly on the stern.

I imagine holding the tiller loosely with the tips of my fingers, sails sensuous and curving billowing out, with my thoughts, like ruffled water, trailing behind.

Remembering a time, when on the rising of the tide, with no hand on the tiller,

Feel Free had drifted out from the shore to be found the next day washed up on some other patch. Complete and intact.

Glenn's pleasure that day was pitched high like the sound of a joyful bird.

"It's here," he'd called. "It's here I can see it." His arms outstretched as he rocked from side to side in the bow of our neighbours boat. I rowed closer, Glenn's tension holding a bubble of laughter as he sighed with relief.

These thoughts are behind my eyes. They are in my bones.

Having once again ended up in hospital it was as if a giant fish with chopping jaws and sharp teeth had wanted to crush and digest me in one greedy gulp. The past mixed in with the present had risen to the surface, almost wiping me out, and I'd become so weak I had had no choice but to hand myself over to the skills of the doctors.

I had allowed my mind and body to do this to me, finding most doctors had little respect for the power of stress and grief.

Now I am beyond those who had imposed the rules.

Before moving out of hospital and into rehab, enough, I finally and clearly had said.

"You doctors had expected to identify the problem, label me, then file me neatly away.

That hasn't worked.

With your numerous tests I've become weaker and weaker.

When I get my strength back in rehabilitation I'm going home. I'll deal with this. I have before and I will again.

I'll do what needs to be done."

We are almost home, turning into our overgrown bush track, to loop around a large old tree.

Nothing has changed.

How often have I lain in bed waiting to hear the first birds in those trees, followed by other long whipping responses. Relieved the night was over, hearing kookaburras laugh my day into being.

Long grasses have overrun the garden, uncared for during my time in hospital.

A distance has opened up between John and me. I need to step outside of what is beyond my control.

The clarity I discovered in my time away is deserting me.

I'm not a part of what is happening.

All families have their particular dynamics. I have no way of changing anything, but I can be here for John. And for Amanda.

I am but a silent partner.

We all have a story, and John's families story is not mine to tell.

The past is not perfect for anyone, perfection would be a dead fish, a life not lived.

I turn my attention to the letters and postcards on the noticeboard, competing with the phone messages I haven't yet had the energy to deal with. A reminder of my time away.

This stay in hospital has been even longer than three years ago.

Yet nowhere near as dramatic.

I have felt pits of grieving that only the grieving can know, taking me to the centre of my being.

We just have to keep on moving.

Yes, I need to keep on moving.

Friends may ask where I've been.

"I've been on a sabbatical" I'll say.

According to the dictionary a sabbatical is the seventh year, when the Israelites were to cease tilling the soil, release debtors, and free the slaves.

I am clearer about the connection of my mind and body than I have ever been, after becoming scattered by the actions of others my body had responded.

I'd yearned for things to be different.

In hospital, I had time, away from everyone and everything.

In that clear uncomplicated space, waving bands of light began to appear out of the gloom I'd thrown myself into, breaking open the honey cells of memory.

The bitter and the sweet.

I am home.

I step out of the car. I pick up a simple stone before walking up the steps.

I choose the stone for its shape and its size.

A memento of my return.

John is at work.

I sit in my favourite chair, the scuffed earthy-coloured velvet is familiar to my touch worrying at a split in the cloth the same way that, as a child, I could never keep my tongue away from an aching tooth, no matter how much it hurt.

Sometimes I've had a poor sense of myself, a sense of my slightness as a person, as a soul. When I was in hospital I had time to think about friendships, about laughter, about loss, and about my failures.

All too clearly.

A long time ago, I can't remember where I read it, maybe Rumi, or some ancient poet. Whoever it was, he or she said:

In myth the scarf is said to be the skin of the soul.

I am held in the creeping warmth of being home, with a scarf around my shoulders.

Writing about my life helps me, but exactly how I cannot say. It could hardly be called therapy, but maybe it is a sign of my ongoing awareness of all life can contain.

I hope so.

Because writing does seem to be hurrying me on, leading me to where I hadn't known I needed to go.

I once had a fantasy about Glenn being on his way home.

Long after the *Crusader* disappeared.

I was driving up the mountain behind an orange Kombi-van like the one Glenn's father had driven years ago in which Glenn and Fiona had learnt to drive.

Thinking I could see two men sitting side by side in the front seat.

So sure it was Glenn's father bringing him home, about to turn into my home track, but the Kombi-Van didn't turn, they just kept on driving.

I left blinking, as a shaft of sunlight pierced the car window.

Not flinching, I turned onto our home track

Floating . . .

Thinking . . .

It must be like this at the bottom of the deepest sea.

Would the water feel heavy, yet be clear?

Would I rest on soft powdery sand?

The trees droop in the blistering heat. A storm is on its way. I sit at my computer and I write. And I write. All I need is emerging through my words and my thinking.

To read and to write has saved me before.

And it will again.

John walks into the room to pick up a book. He walks out again.

What do I want? Maybe to cut through the critical silence that has enveloped me since my return.

I'm hungry for a different kind of silence.

Are you still the free spirit who escaped over a fence to get to the beach?

Where is that child who at four years of age had wanted her freedom, so much?

Life is here. I am poised and ready, a smile on my face as John walks back into the room.

Does he want to change the unspoken stalemate we've come to?

Choosing a CD he presses the start button, turns and walks out, not even looking in my direction.

Augustin Barrios Mangore was a composer with a romantic heart.

John Williams once wrote that he had never lost touch with beauty. Picking up the cover of the CD I read the words spoken by Barrios long before he died.

I am a brother to those medieval troubadours who, in their despair, suffered such romantic madness.

'Dreams in the magic garden,' recorded with the sound of birds in the background.

The music playing reminds me of when John and I first met.

John William's guitar is forcing my thinking out of the space I've been locked into for weeks. Moving me into a state of grace and of gratitude in spite of everything.

I am conscious of every note, mindful of the first night with John in his tiny flat in Balmain soon after we met.

Waking to the sound of him playing his guitar as if playing on my heart.

The way, on our first holiday together on Dunk Island, swimming in the water, tiny fish had circled us as the way Barrios music now swims around me.

Is it too late?

Can grief break the back of love?

Years of the good, and the not so good.

Are notes on a guitar strong enough to haul us back to shore?

I sit at my computer, hands resting lightly on the keys. I'm on the threshold of I'm not sure what, but I implore it to stay. Moisture trickles down my spine. I shiver. Nothing has changed. Everything is the way it was yesterday. How could it be different?

Hold tight. Live in the way that feels right.

Let the past lose its way of bringing you undone.

The river will twist and it will turn, and it will change direction and flow between the shadows and the sun.

There are some who would like to know what their future holds.

I'm not one of them.

Having just finished reading a book by Joyce Carol Oates called *Black Water* based on a real life story, told as a fiction. It is of a young woman who leaves a party with a senator she barely knows. After taking a wrong turn in the dark, his car plunges off a bridge, sinking in the lake.

As the young woman is drowning she remembers the words spoken to her by her grandfather a long time ago. The way you make your life, he told her, the love you put into it, that's what love is.

If we could see beyond the choices we make, and be aware of the unseeable, would we then be able to change the course of our lives?

Amanda, John's eldest daughter, is under a great deal of stress, she is now a single parent to young Dominic and Alexandra.

But Amanda has been forced to face a court case over the custody of Dom and Allie. The custody case loomed large in all of our lives, happenings impossible for me to conceive of, and I think, beyond most people's comprehension.

And it was devastating. But the challenge is unsuccessful.

Later, with hindsight John realised the depth of her despair even though she had won.

You could not deny the privacy of Amandas voice at times. She had a place no one else could touch. Then she surprised us all. After winning the right to keep her children, just a few months later she gave them back to their father, and boarded a plane to New York to live with a friend in Brooklyn and work at the Guggenhiem Museum.

A few years later Amanda did return from New York.

This time she is here to stay.

She'd run away trying to avoid the drama her life had become, leaving us all shattered, but she paid a price, and Amanda, I can see, is still paying a heavy price for that crazy time.

She is back, wishing she could change the past, but none of us can.

Amanda loves her children. And they love her. Closer to them when they are with her, soothing their wounds.

Yet, she has returned to a silence so loud, with some, a silence that has become almost impossible for Amanda to find a way beyond.

And we all need family.

Amanda has a job, in charge of a rehabilitation unit at a city hospital, and is talking of further study. Since she was a teenager, she has always enjoyed working with people, once working her school holidays in an aged persons unit, when on leaving school she became a nurse.

My thoughts are of Amanda, and of wishing what had taken place in court was as easy to delete as pressing a button on my computer.

There have been times in our life when all things fell apart. And everyone lost.

What would it be like if you could delete the most distressful events in your life as simply as I can delete unwanted stuff from my computer.

Flick a switch, wipe out everything that has become feral in our world.

There are myths and stories I've been burying myself in lately. Their sound, their rhythm on the page soothes me.

The circle of time can never be broken. The ocean continues to move in rhythm, the tide goes in and the tide goes out. Our breath goes in and our breath goes out. When I had no choice but to dig deep, I was startled by what had opened me to who I might still be.

In the bleakest of times, I learnt, that how I see, and what I see, determines the steps I need to take.

It is so easy to be caught up in the experiences of others, and in touching they leave you with a resonance of both the good and sometimes the not so good. I am calmer this week than I have been, better able to concentrate on what I want to do.

There are times when I sit alone in a café soaking up conversations at the next table. My imagination flares as I infiltrate a moment in their lives to add to mine. I am an ordinary everyday thief in the way I was last week as I walked through the Art Gallery observing the way people look at art as much as enjoying looking at art myself.

Later leaving Sydney behind I drive back down the coast feeling vaguely dispirited, then John Lennon comes on the radio singing *'Imagine'*, and my equilibrium is restored.

I drive on in a happier state of mind, because music can do that for me.

Almost home after my day in the city.

Smoke or mist drifts up in wisps, the way the thoughts in my head have been and still are like those tiny circumstances of life that can end up being too difficult to deal with, or just beyond our reach. Most things begin in the smallest, most simple way.

I greet John, who is planting lettuce and coriander in his vegetable garden, and I walk into the house thinking *whatever it is he's cooking it smells good, and I'm starving.*

John walks into the kitchen saying "How was your time in Sydney?"

I think of how my time seemed to have been everywhere but where I actually was, and I've exhausted myself. Ready to eat my dinner, climb into bed and feel the peace and comfort arriving home gives me.

There is nothing like climbing into bed with your own pillow.

It's late. The phone is ringing

Half asleep, I jump out of bed to pick it up. Silently I hand it to John.

He holds the receiver as if not wanting to hear what he is hearing, and passes it back to me, saying, "You stay here," as he pulls on his jeans, and grabs for a t-shirt.

"Can't I come too?" I ask.

"No," he says as if he's already some where else.

And detached.

"You stay here. I'll ring you when I get there."

He's out the door, into his car, and on his way to Sydney as if on automatic pilot.

My mind slows down enough to feel the shock waves from the place I don't want to visit. Not again.

Despair has swamped Amanda's fragile happiness.

Only last week she gave me a bundle of books, saying she'd read them and she wouldn't need them any more. I have a clear picture of the smile on her face.

There were things that were not usual that day. Andrea Bocelli singing. Amanda buying us the C.D and wanting to share her favourite track.

But Amanda has always been passionate about music. And books.

Amanda waving to us is as vivid as it was, the day we left to drive south.

I can still see the smile on her face.

All of them waving the last time we were together.

Why?

Why would you, Amanda, take your own life when you had appeared to be moving into calmer waters?

I wait for the call.

It's John.

"Can you come? Can you find your way here?"

I lost Glenn. Now John has lost Amanda.

It rubs my heart, leaving me in a blinding absence of light.

For so long nothing had been simple, for Amanda.

There are days when I wish I could fold myself back to the time before the fragments of Amanda's life had begun to unravel, to when the days of each week were no more than a ripple. No longer sure how far back that would need to be.

Losing Amanda the way we did goes deeper than deep.

I walk to the creek where I spend a part of most days building cairns, in a space where nothing seems to have stirred for years. The third creek, as it has always been known became my space to be with me, with Glenn.

And now with Amanda.

I can't begin to describe the hours I've spent building with stones, one stone on top of another. Choosing the right shape and size. Working here in my gumboots soothes me. I pick up a stone to add to the cairns then I choose another before dropping it back into the fast running stream, not the right shape or size.

In persisting beyond the shadows I look for what I can do.

Call life what you will, the eye of things is here winking between the drizzle and the blue hills. The sun begins to shine. Time doesn't stop. The pendulum keeps on swinging. *Let go, let go* and remember Amanda's quirky sense of the ridiculous, and the way her irreligious humour could always break me up. In all the years I had known her she was up or she was down, seldom was there an in-between. But when Amanda was up she could create joy.

Her life had been chaotic at times, creative and, compulsive. Hard, at times, to comprehend. After returning from New York she seemed to find a balance.

But can we ever find meaning in her decision?

Anam Cara *The Wisdom of the Celtic World* by John O'Donahue is the book we bought in Galway, Ireland, having no idea how important it would be to us when we returned with it tucked neatly into our luggage.

Waking this morning, the first thing I did was open *Anam Cara*. I was filled with questions, hoping O'Donohue would offer me answers. Turning page after page I stopped at page 270, where he'd written:

> I like to imagine that death is like rebirth. The soul is now free in a new world where there is no separation or shadow or tears. We can only see death from one side, no one has the experience. Therefore those who did stay can never see the other half of the circle which death opens us to.

Only weeks after losing Amanda I hear Petrea King talking to Margaret Throsby on ABC radio about a place where people come seeking answers from the programs held at *Quest for Life* in Bundanoon.

I'm sad, and I'm confused about everything.

My heart aches. It's all too hard.

Could Petrea be offering a way to save me? From myself? I can't feel anything, all I can do is take care of John. I can't even grieve, and I'm angry.

I will do this program. John and I will do it together.

No sooner is the interview over, and I am in my car, driving up the mountain to Bundanoon, I want to know more, I want to see this place called *Quest for Life* for myself. A few weeks later we are driving back up the mountain to turn into Quest, past gardens that have been there for years.

I'm still angry, but at what, or at who?

We walk up the steps, through the door into what was many years ago a much-used Guest House that has now been totally refurbished. In me I feel a shift.

My anger lifts. This place envelopes me.

And I am surprised.

I turn to look at John. He is deep in conversation with a woman with laughter in her voice. Hearing her, I somehow know that here, I will be safe.

Coming to Quest was the right decision, but can anything satisfy the hunger my heart feels, but myself?

When I lose my internal direction, as I have, a kind of fever comes upon me, putting me outside everything and everyone. This fever that isn't really a fever has been there inside me for weeks.

Arriving at Quest thinking, *why is this place taking me back to the first time I met Amanda, as a chubby, charismatic, laughing twelve-year-old?*

Her joy is present in a space washed clean. For weeks I'd been claimed by the unreality of it all.

But we have arrived. We are here.

When you think you're falling apart, you do what you have to do, yet finding there is no end to the reason people come to sit in what I call the Sacred Circle. Some have lost their bearings, others may have stubbed their toe, and now don't know what to do about it, but most are dealing with a loss of some kind.

The circle is where goodness, sadness, graciousness and angst in all its unexpected forms can touch you with the unity and the presence of Petrea, holding harmony at the heart of what seems to be like a gathering of lost souls.

And so much sorrow is not pretty. Life can be ugly.

But by the end of our time together, you would not recognise this circle as the same people, diverse though they may be, who had arrived on Monday, some thinking *What the hell am I doing here?*

The Quest for Life foundation had been running on a shoestring.

They discovered a dilapidated, ancient Guest House for sale in Bundanoon. Petrea's imagination had taken flight, yet they have not a hope in hell of buying it until a friend suggests they ring a man known to her.

And they do.

He becomes the silent benefactor who has experienced Petrea's work, believing in what she is doing. He helps her buy the property, providing not only the necessary funds, but also helping with the refurbishment, wanting no recognition. The money supplied will be returned to him if it doesn't work out. As the caretakers of Quest Petrca and her partner Wendie will keep the profit to continue their work in whatever way they choose.

On nine acres of beautiful gardens Quest becomes a haven for many.

Petrea's long-held dream is a reality.

John and I participated in the program called *Healing your Life*, in August 2000.

On the completion of the program I remained connected on a voluntary basis then by the end of the year 2000, Petrea had asked me to become a member of the team, ending up working and living in at Quest from Monday to Friday to work on the programs.

Quest is now a part of my life.

Though the programs are much the same in content, Petrea has a way of going to wherever those in the circle need to go on every program. The circle belongs to the participants, each having its own particular energy.

With Petrea at the helm it becomes what it is meant to be, life-changing for the participants.

As it is for me.

A woman called Sally for me stands out.

Her shiny skull is like a beacon, joy resurfacing for her the week she participates at Quest, regardless of the difficulties she has to deal with.

Joy and tears bursting out of her. Her crazy sense of the ridiculous enlivens everyone as tears and black humour sit on the edge of the circle, ready to become a part of it all.

All week Sally hadn't worn her wig or her prosthesis. On the last day of the program she walks into the lounge room to have a coffee, ready to face the future.

Prosthesis and wig in place.

Make-up on and dressed to kill.

"Sally, I hardly recognise you," I say, "but I think I like the real you better without your extra bits and pieces," and we laugh, and we hug one another.

Where, but in being part of Petrea's circle could I have had that conversation?

Twelve months later Quest is out of funds. They are going to have to close down.

All is to be lost.

Heartbreaking for Jenny and her team of women who take such meticulous care of everything, washing, dusting, vacuuming, and arranging fresh flowers by raiding every garden offered to them to make Quest a place of beauty.

What happens here is like music on a river, flowing year after year with all the unexpected possibilities.

A river doesn't fear death

It has an all embracing way of flowing towards the ocean in an ongoing melody.

The way those working at Quest care about what happens from the smallest task to the way Petrea is totally there for each person sitting in the sacred circle.

And Doug, the chef, handling the many different diets requested with a cheeky kind-of-love, part of the humour that is so often present at Quest. Wendy in the book shop, Doug's wife, is central to many things that take place. Lyn, the counsellor, a miracle-maker cares in her way for the participants, taking them to where they may never have expected to go. Quest can hold tears and laughter in the palm of its hand, and both are central to much of what happens in just five days.

The list could go on and on.

The loss of Quest is devastating for Petrea, and Wendie.

But they have no choice.

I am with Julie's the day Petrea's secretary contacts me, asking me to be a part of the last program at Quest. Wanting to pay me a nominal amount, but I don't need to be paid, I am happy just to be there, sad though the day will be.

A massage rooms is turned into a bedroom for me.

For some reason Petrea has insisted that I be there.

One month later Petrea rings to tell me that Quest for Life is on the move again.

"How come?" I say.

A woman on the final program who was an executive of a large bank, arranged a fundraiser day at Cockle Bay, asking those who could well afford to open their wallets and their cheque books, to come and hear Petrea speak.

This woman who was suffering from cancer had not long to live told her story.

She and Petrea each telling their story had raised enough money for Quest to take the chance of opening again. Her time at Quest had not taken away the cancer, but it had healed her life in other ways that had made her determined Quest would be there for others when she was no longer here.

My time at Quest has not only saved me, it has been the saving of John and I.

An epiphany arrives, the miracles grow. The silent benefactor has recently gifted the Quest property to Quest foundation—forgiving the loan.

Quest will now expand in ways yet unknown.

I can but imagine Petrea and Wendie Thinking: "We can't help everyone, but everyone can help someone."

Arriving home from Quest late Friday afternoon, it isn't long before I'm climbing into bed, then to wake the next morning to the promise of a day working in the garden.

I dig the dirt beneath a sky that is like an endless blue canvas.

I watch birds being as territorial as humans can be, dipping in and out of the bird- bath. The morning has arrived without a hint of the expected change in the weather.

Between what I want life to be and what it is has become, I look for answers in the midst of what at times has felt like a pile of rubble. Last night I looked to the west watching scarlet leaking into ribbons of gold laying across the top of the mountain seeming to push against the sky.

I hum between closed lips, holding close the energy of Glenn, and of Amanda, both out of reach on a day ticking with summer.

I drink in the stillness. I know happiness will come. And it will go.

Surrounded by green, yellow, blue, orange, persimmon, shades of white, and even magenta. Like a bower bird I look beyond the grey of yesterday.

I remember Kristian bouncing with joy blowing out his birthday candles.

Kristian that day was five.

Once, driving him back to Sydney after a holiday at the farm, he rattling on non-stop as five-year-olds do, saying,

"Will you be lonely, Omi, when I go home and back to school?"

"Sometimes Kristian, but we had a great time this week."

With a frown on his face he said, "My dog gets lonely when I go to school. Can you tell Mummy when we see her today that I need to take him to school, with me?"

Back then my joy was as uncomplicated and as simple as a five-year-old wanting answers to his questions.

The way I want Julie, my youngest daughter, to be who she can be.

Why would a passionate, creative person like Julie who in the past has achieved so many things, now be overcome by such overwhelming anxiety.

My heart reels with angst, and with *love*.

But is it enough?

Yet in my time at Quest I'm finding a balance.

A balance between what I can do for Julie, and what I can't do.

Today I'm like a cat on a hot tin roof.

Wanting to cut my life into little pieces, and rearrange it the way I would like it to have been.

My computer has crashed, my printer has gone crazy.

A grown-up Kristian has sourced me a new computer.

And a laser printer that works. I pull my dressing gown around me thinking about everything, and nothing. My mind and my body has taken action, catapulting me into a pool of stillness.

A pot of purple geraniums are on the window-sill.

My laptop stands open on the table waiting for words.

I stare at the screen, and what little I write, I erase.

My garden today has gone from being thick with blue forget-me-knots, and parts of it are a waiting to be filled. This year I'll throw nets over the fruit trees, hoping the birds will leave some fruit for us. Nothing is stirring, except for the buzzing of a couple of drowsy blowflies on the window sill. Is my life to be as simple as this?

Whatever happens, I want to enjoy the everyday things, the way today I think, w*hat will I cook tonight* imagining the colours and the look of what I'll create for dinner and how luscious it will look on the plate. Gathering food out of our garden, thinking of children and grandchildren.

Happiness is always worth itemising.

I've driven home after a couple of days in Sydney, when out of the far distant past I received a phone call from Glenn's friend Ken.

After twenty-six years.

Having moved away from the river I had lost touch with Glenn's friends. It has been a long time since we left the river for the inner city. *How did he find me?*

Ken was the same age as Glenn the last time we were all together. Twenty three.

And it seems like yesterday.

Twenty-six years after Glenn's disappearance Ken was determined to find me, his friend's mother, sit down and have a coffee.

Calling into the village's tiny Post Office, he had asked the postmaster if he knew me. "She lives close to here," Ken says. She had a son who was my friend and who disappeared on a yacht in the Bay of Bengal. She has two daughters, one called Fiona, and the other called Julie."

"Yes, I know her" the Post Master said. "I think she's a poet. But I can't give you her personal information."

That day synchronicity was alive and well.

In telling a colleague about going to the Post Office Ken, was surprised to have him say "I've met her, I heard the story from my wife, we have her phone number."

Walking into the coffee shop in the village that day I look at a man sitting in a cubicle reading the paper, trim in his jeans and white T shirt, a head of close-cropped white hair. A Georgio Armani look. That can't be him. Good-looking, but too old. Walking outside I let my eyes roam the outdoor terrace looking for the young man I came to meet, and the Georgio Amani look-alike walks out of the coffee shop to tap me on the shoulder, saying,

"I wondered if I would recognise you. I would have recognised you anywhere."

Sliding into the booth I feel unsure.

I look across the street to the pots of flowers lining the footpath outside the general store, and they almost spill in a sudden gust, as a flurry of papers and leaves fly up into the air like tiny unattached kites.

Coffee ordered. Food is chosen. And the past sits down beside us.

There is a realness to the connection and I feel contagiously happy.

Ken calling me by my first name seems quite natural.

I laugh.

"You must have a good memory Ken," I say kissing him lightly on the cheek.

"When I told the others I'd spoken to you they wanted to meet with you too, we're all over the place these days. From Palm Beach to the far South Coast. And a couple are interstate or overseas."

Telling me that when they did get together, the talk had always come around to Glenn.

And sailing on the river.

"Do you remember us as that scruffy bunch sitting around that big old table after we came in from sailing? The table you bought for fifty dollars in the second-hand shop, we heaving it down the old stone steps by the side of the house."

I'm surprised at what he is remembering.

"Do you remember us doing that? That table was a heavy bugger."

The food came, coffee poured, memories run wild. So much to talk about.

Never before had I talked with Ken in this way we do today.

The sun is everywhere, the air is clear. My happiness is huge.

His friends had missed him too. Glenn was still important to them.

Oh! How sweet this is. And will always be for me.

I ache with the sweet edge of what we share when we finally meet, making plans to catch up again soon.

"Do you remember wishing me good luck," he said as we said goodbye, "and a good life in whatever I did?"

Home, I walk out onto the deck, my thoughts spinning, and something in me is opening out in the way the dancing dervishes do.

Glenn gave meaning to his short life, for he had a freedom of the *heart*.

Quietly comfortable with who he was, and what he had wanted to do.

His many friends had buzzed around our home by the river the way flies buzz around a honey pot, yet Glenn could have been seen as a solitary person.

But he wasn't.

In my dream last night a wind-torn lake was seen through the limbs of trees.

Thrashing.

Our lake *Swan Lake*.

Glenn hanging out over the side of a small sailing boat. His feet gripping the stirrups to balance against the heavy gusts.

I'd sensed his laughter in the dream rather than heard it.

Glenn was having fun.

Today John and I are off to Vipassana with little idea of what it will be, other than hours and hours of silence. A ten-day retreat at Blackheath we are about to explore.

This morning I had the weirdest experience.

I looked down into the valley, feeling but not hearing the wind in the trees, it was as if I were the trees, as if I were the sun on the bark and the movement of the leaves, even the silvery green tufts of the weeds by the pathway.

I was not separate from.

I look into the garden at the spindly stems of plants that rise fresh every year outside the sunroom window, tiny birds hanging off the swaying stems.

Swaying and sucking at purple tube-like flowers.

Fluttering and sucking at the same time.

Wings flapping, hovering as they feed on the salubrious juices.

It is time to pack the last few things into my knapsack. Before putting my wallet in my bag I open it at the photograph I always carry with me, of a brother and two sisters.

Julie in the first and possibly the last dress she ever made.

Fiona in a simple wedding dress made at Design School by a close friend.

Glenn in a white open-necked shirt stands between them. His hands on their shoulders, looking directly at the camera.

His sisters looking to him in an aura of joy.

Laughter the day of her wedding had lightened hearts filled with tenderness.

Life at that time had been tenuous for us all, first with the family break-up and, then with Fiona suddenly deciding to marry, Glenn about to travel overseas with no idea how long he would be gone.

Here I am writing this as if I were still by the river with Glenn, Fiona and Julie.

But it is all past tense.

You did.

We did.

It's all hindsight.

At Vipassana we are about to learn a technique of meditation that goes back to the time of Buddha. "I must be crazy, John," I say, "I haven't been silent for ten days in my life."

Now in the blue, blue mountains as yet another village slips past.

"On our way to Nirvana," John says, with a sideways grin.

"Together and yet apart" voicing our common thoughts.

"You know we can't even make eye contact once the retreat begins"

"Well?" he says. "I don't know about you, but I can't wait to get started."

Each valley we pass is deeper and greener, each ridge a little bit higher as we slide past on the freeway. Big printing white on green . . . Leura . . . Katoomba, the home of The Three Sisters. It's as if it's the first time I've seen these names.

A church spire. Then another. Rows of craft shops serving Devonshire teas, and the inevitable petrol pumps. The Hydro Majestic had been tarted up for the millennium. Earthworks are everywhere. The mountains are being uncovered. New roads look stark naked, wounded, and in spite of the devastation I feel a surge of excitement at what's to come.

My decision was right.

"You don't have to come," John had been saying for weeks. I, overcome by the will I, won't I, syndrome. "Either do it or don't," he, in frustration, had finally said.

And we are almost there.

The energy between us today is different from what it can be.

The nearness of sitting in the car cruising along the expressway makes me happy.

A feeling I sometimes struggle to retain.

Away from the everyday, together, driving towards silence.

John glances at me with a look of questioning surprise, as if aware of my thinking.

His eyes turn back to the freeway. I look at him, then two short bursts of looking again. Grey, grey eyes a strong nose, and the curve of a skull as bare as the day we met. Maybe not as handsome at close quarters, but the total is greater than the parts.

But John at times has been too charismatic for his own good.

The big print name, Blackheath, flashes overhead as we skim past the exit, John brakes too fast, the car skids into the safety lane of the freeway.

I grip his arm.

His startled "shit" hits my ear. We come to a halt.

Slowly we take the next turn to catch the first glimpse of a Vipassana sign through the trees.

Our eyes meet.

"Well?" I say.

John chooses his words carefully. "Not what I expected, but what's new?"

"Has anything ever been what we expected?"

Looking towards the valley, beyond the cluster of buildings and simple gardens, we see earthy pathways wind through the trees. Two young people are lumbering their backpacks to where we've been told to gather.

A motley bunch, dressed for comfort.

Not a clue what the amenities are to be.

And Blackheath can be freezing.

"What do you think?" I say "How sparse do you think our sleeping arrangements will be?"

I have come prepared for anything.

There are to be about seventy people.

A young woman on the far side of the large deck stands out. I had noticed her walking from her car. All these years later she is an adult. And she's tall. This young woman's mother had made inroads into our life many years ago.

Back then had nothing to do with this young woman. She will not recognise me. It has been a long time, but she may recognise John.

Silently chanting, I'm here with myself, for myself, and not with anyone else, no matter who.

We share the night meal, the women in one dining room, the men in another. After the first getting-to-know-you meal we will move into silence. I sign my forms, and give my details. Surprised I'm not in a dormitory, but in a room with a shower and a toilet. I can't believe my luck.

The sound of a bell is calling us to dinner, to chat before the silence descends.

No reading or writing. No anything.

Other than silence.

But not to read or write. Wow! That is something else.

I follow the sound along the pathway marked for women only in a world that has lost all human sound.

It's to be a continuum of eating, sleeping and meditating.

Lining up for meals is like being back at boarding school. But this time it's been my decision. Served a bowl of pungent vegetable soup I cut a large chunk of bread, and slap it with oodles of butter.

Who knows when or what the next meal might be? I sit at a significantly long stool beside a table. I hope the meditation I'm about to learn will cut through the chatter in my mind.

Why would I do this to myself?

The Dalai Lama once said all things originate in the mind.

Thinking, *I must be crazy to be doing this,* as the room fills with women of differing ages.

A Vipassana retreat, though similar at this early stage to the Quest for Life program, could never be the same. On the first day at Quest many participants look as if they are thinking, *what the hell am I doing?*

Wishing to be anywhere but where they are.

For some, this is not the first time here, but I find it hopeful that they have chosen to return.

Introductions. "Hellos. Where are you from?" Nothing too heavy.

"Hi!" a woman in her fifties says. This cap of shiny black hair with smiling eyes sits down beside me.

"I'm Jana, I saw you arrive. You're game coming with a partner"

"Not really. Doing it separately, but later we can share the experience."

"Good luck," another says. "I came with my partner last time. I had been before. the first time for him, spending all my time worrying about how he was handling it.

I'd never do that again."

"I nearly didn't come," I say, "but I'm glad I'm here."

I think I am.

"Who talked you into it?" Jana says.

"John, my partner, has been talking about doing it, but he didn't talk me into it."

"I don't like to miss out on anything."

"Are you working?" Jana says.

Not waiting for an answer she tells me she's a nurse. "I'm over my job big time."

"It's crazy these days, the system's stuffed. Yet there are good people who want to do a proper job and they can't?" She's hoping to be zapped with an epiphany about her next move.

"You never know," I say.

"And to answer your question, Jana, I landed in hospital, had to give up what I'd loved doing. Working with Aboriginal women and children."

"Then later I ended up working at Quest on the programs at Bundanoon."

"Petrea King is quite a woman," Jana says. "I've heard about her."

"I work on the team for the three core programs, Jana, and in answer to your question I have retired."

"Life throws some unexpected twists, and I became part of the good things that happen at Quest. Working in retirement hasn't left me a lot of time for things like Vapassana."

This week my life will be in my face as never before.

After hours of meditation and sitting on the floor I'm in agony. My body is stuffed. And I've barely begun.

In the first break the teacher tells us we can meditate for the next session in our bedroom if we choose to.

I'm off and away before the teacher has finished speaking.

Back to my room.

Knocking on my door is Elise. In charge of the women's section.

To bring me back to what they call the Temple.

"But we can meditate for the next session in our room." I'm almost crying

"That's right, but first you return to the Temple."

"I'll have to sit on a chair Elise, I'm in agony."

"At the end of the night you ask the teacher," is her response.

I have done this to myself, thinking I want to do it the way the others are.

sitting on the floor, but not for so many hours.

Later I still resist asking for a chair.

I walk on pathways liquefying into blackness, wanting my body to feel normal, thinking *this is all too enveloping.* Relieved to reach my cabin and leave the tar-like night behind.

I turn on the light, close the door, wrap myself in a blanket and fall into bed.

Buttocks aching, everything aches. I want to sleep. I want my own bed.

Sitting from early morning to late at night on the floor.

I must be an idiot.

By the next morning Elise had placed a meditation stool at the spot I had been allocated. Better, but still excruciating.

After breakfast Elise knocks on my door.

Saying, "Would you like a chair?"

"I would love that," I say.

I do get into the swing of things. It's not easy. But I will do it no matter how hard it gets. On the ninth day the silence is over. Strange to be talking, actually looking into people's eyes, and Jana, the woman I had spoken to before entering the silence is the first person to approach me.

"How was it for you?" she asks.

Jana had wanted to leave but they talked her into staying.

"I didn't want to leave Jana, but I didn't find it easy."

"Can I pour you a glass of water? I'm dying for a coffee" she says, and adds "How come at your age you work at Quest?"

I don't want to talk about the why.

Jana is unusually persistent, giving me no option.

"It was three weeks after we lost Amanda, John's daughter, when I was listening to a conversation on ABC radio about a program called Quest for Life. Back then I was feeling dark about many things. I lost my son. He was crewing on a yacht that has never been found."

"Where?" She says.

"What do you mean?" Thinking, *what does that matter?*

"Where was the yacht?"

"In the Bay of Bengal." Wishing I'd avoided this conversation.

"When did this happen?" she asks.

"In December,1977."

Jana looked at me for such a long time before saying, "I don't believe this. My friend Robyn was on that yacht, with her partner Richard. They left their own yacht in the Maldives. They were crewing on the *Crusader* because they'd run out of money. They left the *Crusader* in Galle before it set sail. Robyn had refused to sail on it. Richard had refused to leave. Finally he did disembark. Robyn had had a premonition, she often has them, a premonition something was going to happen to the *Crusader*."

I am left hurtling down a familiar track back to Christmas *1977*.

Jana quickly saying, "Ring Robyn. She lives in Melbourne. She's a nurse like me. Richard now lives on his boat in Sydney."

"No!" I finally say.

"It wouldn't be right to ring Robyn after so many years. You can tell her what has happened. That you met me. But the contact has to come from her."

A month later Fiona calls to ask if I've heard anything.

"No," I say.

"Not anything Mum?"

"I haven't." Then I ring Jana. I have her mobile number.

How can you go to a retreat and meet a woman among seventy people, and have that same woman be the first person to speak to you when you come out of the silence, to make this connection?

Robyn had tried to get in touch but she had the wrong number.

After speaking to Jana I make contact. The outcome, a few months later is that I go to Melbourne to meet her. Taking a slow trip down by train, expecting to have a meal with Robyn, but she insists I stay with her in South Melbourne.

Walking into her apartment is like walking into familiar territory. I give a strange little laugh, not a true laugh, more like a cry, surprised at my reaction on meeting the last person to be with Glenn before he sailed away. She is so inviting of me, someone she had never met. Such souls do exist and our friendship begins.

If Fiona hadn't asked the question, I would have let it go. Questions being asked by Jana, then by Fiona, have set in motion a chain of improbable happenings.

Meeting Robyn, the last person to be with Glenn on the *Crusader* before it sailed out of Galle Harbour, is still hard to believe.

Behind my thoughts another world waits. Is the mystery never to leave? The invisible at times seems visible, the way Glenn and Amanda are sometimes closer than they ever were.

Why do we harm one another the way we sometimes do?
When kindness is so easy.
And friendship, true friendship, the gift.
And death, a road I am yet to take.

My memories today are of my mother. And my father.

My father died in 1997. Nine months later, on 15 September 1997, my mother took her leave. Never before have I been aware that in caring for us they had been love on wheels, ready to go to wherever they were most needed.

My parents married at seventeen and eighteen. A choice made by others when it was discovered I was about to make my presence felt.

Passion, for my parents, had had its consequence.

And the consequence was me.

With young parents who were living through the Depression I didn't experience an easy outward expression of *love*. My mother, after I was born, was in and out of hospital time after time, leaving a young father to care for me in the midst of demanding new life, struggling to support them through those difficult years.

With great foresight, he became a budding entrepreneur, opening one of the first hamburger shops of his era. An older friend, a craftsman, had offered to outfit the shop for them, suggesting my father pay him back when he'd accumulated the necessary funds.

They worked long hours.

For me, it was a time of separation.

Sent to boarding school the week before my eighth birthday.

Hamburgers—hamburgers in an ice cream scoop.

I learnt to scoop raw mince rather than ice cream.

Filling trays with layers and layers of raw meat to be cooked in the window of the shop where passers-by could watch my father place cooked mince between toasted buns, with tomato, beetroot, lettuce, cucumber and fried onions.

Oozing with tomato sauce.

Still remembering those never-ending trays of scooped raw meat and . . . the gypsies.

I loved the gypsies.

Coming into the shop, giving me a shivering sense of danger.

To add to my excitement I'd been warned gypsies stole children, particularly little girls. Every time they came in I would place a sixpence in the palm of the hand of each of them, men and women. Have them tell me the most wonderful stories of what my future one day could be.

Mind-boggling for a seven-year-old.

Smiling faces, untidy hair, colourful people filled with irreverent laughter. In a scared kind of way, I had hoped that if the gypsies really did steal little girls . . . they just might steal me.

But they didn't. I was sent to boarding school.

Years later, beyond the loneliness I'd felt as a child, I could see myself when Glenn, Fiona and Julie were young, not really knowing how to show *love* in the way I would have wished to.

Was it like pushing against the wind?

Unsure about what I was doing, knowing deep down that *love* has no limits, but it did need to be acted upon. *Love* had need of a voice.

How else can it be known?

When my mother was in the nursing home, losing her sight, she sensed my arrival. No Hello darling, how are you? as was usual. Just reaching out to offer her most important news.

"I'm going to God, and I'm starting right now," was what she said.

Kissing her hello, I didn't know quite how to respond.

But I said, "You sound happy, Mum."

"It's a good place," was her response. "Here is good, but where I'm going is better."

In the last days of my mother's life I could see she was not just dying.

She was, ever so graciously, living her dying.

Tears of sorrow can reconstitute a heart laid bare.

Yet, through my tears I am connected to those no longer here.

The last couple of years of my parents' lives were the most demanding.

Laughingly once saying to me, "We are way past our use-by date, darling."

And for them there was a truth in what they could so easily joke about. On her last days my mother had abstracted herself from everything. And everyone.

Except me.

The nurse moved her out of the ward into a room surrounded by windows looking onto a garden with plants and trees and closely clipped lawns. The nurse left and I closed the door to fossick for candles.

Turning off the harsh overhead lights I circled the candles around the room.

Then I lit them.

I sat beside my mother. I held her hand.

I breathed in her rhythm, until all breathing had ceased.

They had occasionally talked of their God, but not of organised religions. That day my mother had clearly made her decision, leaving me to wonder what my father would have thought at such a clear-sighted choice. He was of an era when men made the decisions.

My father had left first, giving my mother the chance to make this decision for herself.

In a candlelit room, the nurses prepared her body, washing and dressing her, and talking to me, and to one another as if they were on hallowed ground.

Two gentle ghosts performing the last rites.

Death had tapped me on the shoulder, and it had tugged at my heart.

The nurses left, leaving me to wait for Fiona and Julie who were driving down from the city to farewell their grandmother. Later, when they were leaving to drive back to the city, it seemed as if a door had closed on them.

Before they were ready.

The importance of my children's grandparents and great-grandparents to them, was shown by the way Fiona, Julie and Kristian spoke at their final celebrations.

John read Kristian's words to his great-grandmother. Kristian was too shy.

I don't know many who meet or get to know their great grandparents. I was lucky enough to do both. I have fond memories of spending time in Centennial Park with them as a child. A special memory of feeding the ducks asking If I could take one home Grandma always replying, I don't think your mother would like that. Our ventures to the park would be a ritual I looked forward to every week. They were always interested in the things I did. Always encouraging me to do my best. And above all my grandmother telling me I must be true to myself.

Yet there are things we forget to say in the unthinkingness of our everyday. Thin-limbed feelings, words and thoughts you wish you'd expressed when those you have loved are still with you.

But today my eyes are tightly shut against what I cannot reclaim. With a trace of a smile I have the joy of knowing I have lived my life with a fist full of gold.

And I had not always known this.

Roles were reversed in the final year of caring for my parents.

But I was still their child.

Glenn, Fiona and Julie, their grandchildren.

Kristian, their great-grandchild.

Sitting by her bed that day I pulled apart a rose, petal by petal, to sprinkle over my mother's body.

Circling her head was a crown of flowers.

Daylight crept in.

I drove to the harbour to watch the sun rise and sit on a blurred horizon, holding the softly bruised colours of my thinking.

My mother had been there for me for all my life.

She knew I would be with her until the end. And I was.

Driving home, thoughts held close about the way my mother had taken her leave.

Her final gift to me.

The air around me is clear—infinitely clear.

Like water sparkling in the sunlight.

And children laughing.

Grief is not separate from.

It is, but a part of.

Today I walk beside the sea in a solitude that is new to me.

I let the rhythm of the sea in.

A quietness settles. Less to say. More time to be.

When to? When not to?

There comes a time, or maybe there is an age, when you slip off the radar screen of the everyday, and are more aware of the changes that are part of being a family, feel the loss, yet live with it rather than expecting it to be different.

In the reflection of my ancestors, I'm aware of the simple lineage I inherited that has given me the strength I needed.

My maternal grandmother's words are with me still:

> If you are really determined to achieve your heart's desire, you have to believe first in yourself. Then there is a point when you move beyond that. You persevere beyond what hurts. It can be painful, yet if you believe in what you are about to do, you will achieve it.

John is driving north to spend the night with Melanie, his youngest daughter, who is moving to Perth to live. Time for her to take the opportunities being offered and get on with her life. She has what looks to be an exciting job, and it seems to be quite diverse.

Her only child, Kasarn, is now settled with her little family.

All those years ago, Melanie lost Clayton, her young husband to cancer. Clayton who was a rebel with the heart of an angel.

And Kasarn was so young.

It is time Melanie had a life that is hers. She has cared in every way, and still does, for Kasarn and her grand-children, but she needs to take charge of her life.

Time to reach out and take the opportunities she has created for herself. Let go of the losses, that at times we all face.

Melanie needs to live her life.

The years are merging, but there are changes, changes brought about bit by bit, simple steps which in themselves do not seem to be important, and yet random happenings have all too often disconnected me from what could have been.

But here I am about to head off for my early morning walk to the third creek. I do this in unbearable heat. I do this in the icy cold.

I do this no matter what.

Today in this heat even the birds have ceased to warble.

Shrouded by the noisy silence of the rainforest, I lean back to rest against one of the huge mossy boulders with a strong sense of Glenn, his laughter skittering, weaving its way in and around the trees, but his light is somewhere else.

In the creek I build cairns to memory.

Reaching into the fast running water I collect pebbles to add to the cairns. Rock by rock, pebble by pebble. It doesn't matter what presidents and prime ministers do, or how scary the world has become, this creek has been my link to life.

And death.

Birds will fly free and seasons will change.

I reach into the creek and my gumboot makes a sucking sound as I pull one foot out of the soft mud. Glints of sun spill through the canopy.

The surface of the creek shivers.

Today is to be a scorcher.

The next day driving to Sydney to farewell Fiona my air conditioning clapped out, I wished I could be in the coolness and comfort of the creek, and yet I need to spend time with Fiona before she leaves for overseas.

Spend time with Julie, too, who has been through a challenging time.

For a few years her resilience has been tested, yet I am quietly confident that she will do what she has to do and she will not be found wanting.

We all have things in our life we need to reclaim, and Julie will find her way.

For no reason at all, Julie bought me a present saying, "I hope you'll like it, Mum."

Finally giving it to me and saying, "You may not like it."

It was the word Faith in brass letters. And it was beautiful.

I placed it above the fireplace where I light three candles every morning in front of the tiny sculpture Fiona brought back from Sri Lanka. Now I light four candles every night behind the word Faith.

I have more faith in Julie than she has in herself lately.

To come to a breaking point has been more than just difficult for Julie, but her spirit, and her quirky nature, is beginning to surface.

I remember how hard it once was to believe the sun would still shine, that good things could still happen.

But the sound in Julie's voice is what I've been waiting to hear.

Catching up with Fiona I'd wanted to forget she was about to fly across the ocean as Glenn once had. As we shared a glass of wine, she sat gazing at me for a long time.

Then said, Mum, "Why so sad?"

I dragged my thinking out into the open where Fiona wanted it to be.

It's difficult to hide feelings, your voice gives you away. Everything I damn well do can give me away.

And just as well.

Yet way beyond here the war in Iraq is escalating.

Since September 11 2001 I have been lighting candles as a daily ritual of hope.

And now if I forget to light the candles, John does.

A wave of memory hits, my thoughts are in full flow, carrying a sense of joy in spite of the news on the radio of the most recent disaster in the world.

Giving me all the more reason to use my imaginative eye in making a garden to live with. To make my plot of earth more beautiful seems to be the least I can do. And imperfect though it may be it will be lovable, with plenty of room for my imagining.

When I pull the weeds out of the uncared-for overgrown patches I come upon a crocus, a perfect white flower, and my heart leaps.

I cherish the survival of these plants that have been almost lost the way the lily I planted disappeared at the end of its first season as if it had never existed, yet each year, at the same time, it reappears. And it continues to surprise.

Death of a plant, as in life, is not sinister.

It is our common denominator.

How strange memories can be.

Activating, recalling, enlarging and reducing events and occasions, bringing back facts and fictions, mistakes and misgivings. A repository of my jumbled fears is now activated by Fiona being about to board a plane.

Once I had instant access to fear that I found all too easy to locate, balanced on the edge of my thinking. Aware of how I'd feel for three days before either Fiona or Julie were to fly across the ocean. Fiona asking why I was so sad gave me the chance to talk about what I needed to share.

I could relax, my anxiety was gone.

Walking back from the creek, having stayed longer than usual I feel strange, almost overcome.

Was it the dream I had last night?

Or just the day?

Standing on the deck I look into the house, enjoying what John and I have finally created. Yet I have a reluctance to be at home today, wanting to jump into the car and drive away.

A need to be somewhere else. I need to let go of *what if.*

But I look into our house, holding the chaos of my obsessions.

Books and papers spill all over the place. I've been off the planet for weeks, my head filled with ideas that weave and loop carrying me into stories that touch into, and take me beyond, the shadows of my thinking.

Books, films and plays are what have always opened me to others.

And to myself.

John has found ways to live with my idiosyncratic way of being that can be as unpredictable as the crazy world we live in, and he continues to create even more bookshelves in his effort to keep my chaos contained.

Last night's dream sits on the surface of my mind.

Love, and forgiveness, I'm discovering is what life's about, and it is becoming central to my everyday. I haven't always been able to forgive the actions others may have taken, but as time goes by I am able to forgive the person who took the action.

Never-the-less, it does take two to tango, and without clear communication I have no choice but to let the situation be. To say *sorry* for some is less than easy.

Out of fear? But fear of what?

This dream has lodged in the cells of my body. An echo of a lost, yet sheltered kinship, leaving me to question whether one world can contain glimpses of another?

At 1.20 in the morning I jump out of bed. I walk downstairs to scribble in my journal as if my life depended on it.

I wake, Glenn this morning in my thinking. I sitting beside what remains of last night's fire, hit by a snap of winter in the middle of summer, the embers still glowing as if the night of the soul is upon me.

A dream, just a dream brings hope, for me, and the chaotic world we are all living in, and just a dream has taken me beyond anything I could ever have experienced.

Has Glenn been the beacon, coming to me with the clarity of a gentle gong.

At 1.45 16 May 2004 I have come to have some understanding of what at times had consumed me.

Glenn for me will forever be reflected in Fiona, in Julie, and then through each of us, in Kristian.

There is an opening out, never before realizing this in the way I do this morning.

There is a poem by Rumi in the left hand corner of every page in this journal, and on this page the poem is:

> Though we seem to be sleeping
> there is an inner wakefulness
> that directs the dream
> and that will eventually startle us back
> to the truth of who we are.

The most ordinary, and the most extraordinary has arrived to peel away the layers. I not aware of the miracle unfolding.

To others it may not be a miracle, but to me it is.

Order can come out of chaos. This I do know.

The dream is the miracle, not the destination.

The energy it brings envelopes me, holds me close, giving me what in reality will always be a mystery.

What I write is who I am.

And even years later *grief* is not what you might expect it to be, it can be distant or it can be as close as your next breath.

Taking you by surprise in its intensity. It can almost obliterate you.

When my mother and my father died, I could do what needed to be done.

Losing Glenn I lived the totality of the loss.

In writing Grief is a river I now know, you never lose those you love.

After the storm, and after my time in the creek this morning I stand on the deck to watch the day arrive. When I leave this life I want to drift the way clouds drift, drift down grain by grain beneath all the currents moving around the vastness of the ocean.

This thinking is like a magnet, pulling at me.

I walk back across the deck and down the steps. I climb into my car to drive in a direction that today had not been my intention.

I head for Seven Mile Beach. The beach I claimed as mine.

I pull up in an empty space and park the car.

The sand is hot and dry. With my lips partly open I take in a deep breath. The beach seems to expand. sensing the smells and the sounds of the sea.

Why am I here, and why today.

I climb up a sand dune, then I slide down. The suction of soft sand is pulling at me as the beach below seems to fall away.

A hot breeze blows in my face. The cold ocean spreads out before me but I am scorched, sweat evaporates in the salty air. Space splits asunder. The sky goes on and on. Behind me the sun flicks out tongues of fire.

I don't want to be here gazing at the sea. I want to forget.

I force myself to stay.

I face the void.

Feeling the heat of the sand, I hesitate.

Who could have anticipated, or imagined, or been forewarned, that after so many years I could still feel like this?

My feet slip and I want to scream but my mouth is plastered shut.

The blue of the sky in front of me appears to be rising out of the deep, deep sea.

My long-gone thoughts are of a time when my life had been lost to the stillness of a silent ocean, leaving me with . . .

Where are you Glenn? Who could you have become?

Out of the ether last night a dream came floating in. It was not to be lost.

In darkness I walked downstairs. I sat. And I wrote.

Glenn in his quiet way seemed to know exactly what he wanted to do.

Now he lives in the air I breathe.

There are so many stories the ocean could tell, but I can't turn this into a sad story.

The ocean is larger than I am.

The beach is empty.

Sun touches the skim of waves.

Way out.

I kick off my sneakers, peel off my jeans and my shirt to run the last few yards before diving in and swimming out through the breakers, kicking my legs and flapping my arms to stay afloat. Waves break, folding into the horizon, pulling water across the sand. Gathering strength they rear up, and they roll in time and time again.

A turquoise transparency.

Precious.

Fleeting.

Then sweeping away, pulling one way and then another.

I slip beneath the waves to swim back to the beach. I walk out dripping. My eyes closed, hot air surrounds me.

Grabbing for my clothes, I wander up the beach to lie face down spread-eagled on the sand, thinking of the hours we'd once spent bending over shallow pools among the rocks the year we'd taken a month to drive across the centre of the state, camping all the way, then on to Adelaide where Glenn's father had sailed in a regatta.

Driving all the way back along the road that rimmed the ocean to our home by the river. Camping each night on beaches where crabs scurried among the rocks, crawling across the sand, and burrowing in.

Back then rock pools were sheets of glass, windows to another world.

I've been on Seven Mile Beach for hours. I pick up my sneakers, shake them pouring out every grain of sand, asking that this night be over.

The sea is black, gashed by foam hitting the shore.

Was Glenn scared when light and dark mingled, rolled and rose with the sea?

Moonlight dances on the ocean. To dive into the sea today was like passing through a curtain to a major event.

The sand is cold.

I rub my feet to warm them.

I could be at home.

I could be asleep in my comfortable bed.

It is time and though I cannot see him . . . he is here.

Somewhere.

Grief is my river.

In the unexpected I've found a balance. In building my Cairns in the rainforest.

In my wildest imagination I could not have called that creek a river.

A place of boulders, rocks and trees, and green, green moss, a space where I can be with what no longer is.

Others may have a sacred corner, or a shelf, or a whole room as their sacred space.

I have the rainforest, and the sound of water in the place I have come to love.

Be a part of.

In that creek I caught up with living in the best way I knew how.

There was no way back to the past.

After endless thinking, I'm here sitting on the sand beside the sea. I've been here all night. It is time to go home.

As the sun rises out of the sea I unwind myself, tie up the laces of my sneakers and brush the sand granules off my legs.

I walked a long way last night.

Now I amble back towards the northern end, to the narrow bridge that spans the transparency of a creek flowing into the ocean, filled with schools of tiny fish.

I walk past the children's playground to the café. I sit at a table in the sun, more than ready to soak up the early morning heat.

The night on the beach had been long and chilly.

Waiting for the waitress my thoughts are not of food, my thoughts are of *Love*. And not of that crazy compulsive disorder many have experienced.

That is not the kind of love I'm experiencing. Not today.

A tall gangly young girl with a broad smile walks towards me. A pad and pen in her hand as if taking note of my scrappy appearance. But no, she only wants to take my order. I pick up the menu, flipping past the more fancy possibilities, I order.

I finish my French toast and bacon, and I sip the last dregs of my coffee, trying to remember where I parked yesterday.

I rub my full stomach as I walk to the car.

After a last long last look at the sea I open the car door and slide in, appreciating the coolness of leather.

I turn the key and head for home.

John's car is standing in the driveway below the house. As I walk up the steps and onto the deck he opens the door to greet me. Pleased to see him, I smile.

Even though I am somewhere else, I do kiss him hello.

You look younger today, he says with a grin. Younger than usual, he says.

He chuckles.

I'm puzzled.

I'm not young, I say.

Standing in the sun-filled living room we look at one another then we start to laugh.

I can't stop.

At the beach last night the most terrifying thing was the blackness of the sea.

And now my heart beats too quickly after a night that defies definition.

The tree trunks framed in the doorway look like sculptures.

I want their strength.

I want their sureness.

But one thing I do know is we are not our bodies.

I've known this since the experience landing me in hospital.

I have a body and I have a Spirit.

It comforts me to know that Glenn was life, love, call it what you will, he was more than his body. After having been close to death, I know.

There is nothing to fear.

I discovered this when my body had ceased functioning, my speech became crazy and jumbled, yet there I was in a state of peace I still find impossible to describe.

Beyond understanding.

I had every reason to feel fear.

Yet I hadn't.

To everyone involved it must have been a complete freak-out.

It had nothing to do with courage, it was as if I had no past.

And no future.

A day I'll never forget carried me towards an almost complete recovery.

I was healed.

Surprising everyone. Even the doctors.

If I am not clear in my intention, life as I know it, and want it to be, could become sticky.

It's not meant to be sticky.

Change is the way of things. Nothing is permanent.

I look at what had become fragmented. I look at what I can do, rather than what I can't do, gathering together what needs to be reconnected. If that's not possible I have no choice but to accept what is, do what Glenn had always done.

Take a firm grip on life and not waste any of it.

Glenn would have held life by the tail if he'd needed to.

He lived his twenty-three years well. He knew how to live his life.

And since his disappearance on the *Crusader* he has been my teacher.

A tiny sparrow arrives to perch on the timber railing outside the bedroom, it chirps at me, then flies away.

I'm exhausted. I have no idea what it is I've found.

No.

Not found. The sea and I have set something free.

After my time on the beach, I am lighter, emptier.

And I am different in an ever so distinctly subtle way.

There is no point in staying saddened by the past. I must honour the connection I have, and will always have, here, there and everywhere.

No reason to close anything up tight.

For me everything becomes real when I put pen to paper.

I've sorted myself out as best I could and I've taken chances.

I've opened myself up to things I couldn't have imagined being part of, and as a result I have become more connected to who I want to be.

A few tendrils of hair are sticking to my neck.

The curtains in the room barely stir.

Dust is suspended, luminous and oblique in the filtering light.

I walk upstairs.

Then I pause.

A gust of wind has the curtains framing the window at the top of the stairs fluttering in sensual, undulating folds.

Everything today is out of the ordinary.

Everything after the dream is not the same.

My day is not conforming to anything I have ever felt before.

In the bathroom I close my eyes.

I brush my hand lightly across my face, I feel my forehead, my eyebrows, my nose and my mouth.

I'm as hollow as a sea-shell.

My eyes wide open I catch a glimpse of myself in the mirror, my thin body, and my skinny white arms could so easily snap.

But I come from wiry stock.

Does my soul need *Love* as urgently as I need air?

The uncomplicated *love* the dream had offered has given me a way of being that will blossom regardless of how sad I may feel, or how joyful.

Nothing is lost or forgotten.

Possibility is the secret heart of creativity. True friendship does not wound intentionally. It accepts what is, then no matter how far apart you may be, there is no distance.

That is the power of the kind heart.

We are unique.

And *love,* I believe, is our deepest, truest nature.

Kalyana-mitra, I'd read, means noble friend, and Kalyana-mitra will not accept pretence. Your noble friend will softly and gently confront the blind spot, the spot that you yourself find so difficult to see.

In the past I had railed against being confronted by my blind spot, then in a time of quiet, when the steam had gone out of the situation . . .

I had taken note.

I looked behind the words and saw what I needed to see, realising that the only one who can allow actions or words to wound me is myself.

Nothing to be gained in laying blame, just something to be aimed for.

To disconnect what had once been connected means we all lose.

I now need clear, uncomplicated communication.

All is quiet.

John is downstairs. As I look down into the valley, the weather is about to change.

The silence is pervasive. In the valley the haze created by heat is suspended. The foliage and the trees blur. Climbing into bed in the middle of the day, I wiggle my body burrowing down under the soft cotton covering.

I float into a place beyond sleep.

Hours later I stretch my right leg, hitting my big toe on the end of the bed.

It hurts.

Rubbing it with my thumb and my middle finger, I hear John talking on the phone downstairs. His voice is the residue of a day about to end.

There is a glow.

A glass of apple juice, its golden colour lustrous, sitting on the bedside table under the lamp. John walks up the stairs and into the bedroom, and carefully hands me a cup of steaming coffee.

"I was beginning to believe you would never surface," he says.

I sip at my coffee, but it is too hot, so I nibble at a biscuit, one of those nutty, crunchy kinds.

A florentine dipped in chocolate.

The river is in full flow.

After the dream it was as if I'd let go of a weight I hadn't known I was still carrying. I put the past, and the yet-to-be, in separate, sacred bundles.

No longer do I make predictions of what should, or could not be.

In the dream a benediction of *love* was offered.

And I accepted it.

In turn I am more able to offer the same benediction to those who live in this valley, and to those I love living their lives beyond this valley.

Like butterfly wings of loss, they live in and around me.

One day, they could so easily, just gather together.

As this year comes to an end, I am moving beyond *the river of grief.*

It has kept me afloat.

As have Fiona, Julie and Kristian. And John.

I call to mind Rumi's words in the journal Fiona gave me a long time ago.

> *Let go of days full of wanting.*
> *Let them go without worrying that they do go.*

I am free. And from what?

I am not sure.

THE PRESENT

Not quite straight
a house
an Island's surface carries water's language
less calculated than tides
the twist of autumn lets down the light of winters spoken form and
    force
high above pre-empted words soar into nights fast abiding sense of
    whispered beauty
detailed space surrendered
wind falls under the sun
light leans in from the left
breathes the sweat of dreams
wounded curled up hurtles along a road no longer there
skirts a past now less thought of than soup tins clothes pegs or
    biscuits feathered in the fall of snow
in the early hours slivers of the yet to be spins you aloft
seek life in the slant of morning broken open just around the corner
to reveal the ambient pathways of your sleeping Ghost.

fay marie mcdonald

ACKNOWLEDGEMENTS

Grief is a River, the tangible result of time spent, with gratitude for the friendship made along the way. To the South Coast Writers, especially to Linda Godfrey, who has been my friend and my primary mentor for a long time.

To a great group of writing friends, meeting together most weeks for sixteen years: Linda Godfrey, Andrea Gawthorne, Elizabeth Hodgson, Susan McCreery, Ali Jane Smith and Doreen Lindsay. With the support of these young women this memoir came into being.

My family Glenn, Fiona, Julie and Kristian.

Glenn's father Robert, searching, keeping in touch.

Beth and her family for a safe harbour and a chance to reclaim my life.

Knights Hill, a community of great people.

Friendships, always important.

My time at Wollongong University in the faculty of Creative Arts.

My Aboriginal students and the small miracles I experienced with them.

Sue Woolfe, author of **Leaning towards Infinity**, still one of my favourite books. Mentoring me and telling me I had a voice when I did not know what that meant.

Peter Bishop, the Creative Director of **Varuna Writers House** in Katoomba who believed in the writing and the format I chose.

My five years at **Quest for Life** as a member of a team of wonderful people and the hundreds of participants.

John's children Peter, Amanda, Melanie and their children.

Finally my thanks to John, my final editor, who gave me the space to do what I had no choice but to do and to its completion after it had arrived many years ago in disrupted fragments eventually to become my completed manuscript.

A much distilled essence of a journey with my child.

A journey I had no choice but to take